ALL SOULS

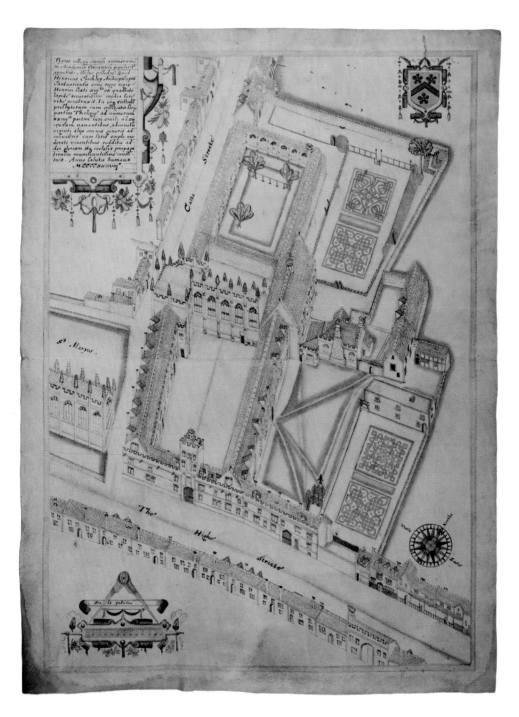

Bird's-eye view of All Souls College in about 1600, known as the *Typus Collegii*,
drawn by Thomas Langdon. *All Souls Archives, Hovenden Maps I, 1*

ALL SOULS

An Oxford College and its Buildings

THE CHICHELE LECTURES
1986

DELIVERED BY

HOWARD COLVIN

AND

J. S. G. SIMMONS

OXFORD UNIVERSITY PRESS

1989

Oxford University Press, Walton Street, Oxford OX2 6DP
Oxford New York Toronto Melbourne Auckland
Delhi Bombay Calcutta Madras Karachi
Petaling Jaya Singapore Hong Kong Tokyo
Nairobi Dar es Salaam Cape Town
and associated companies in
Berlin Ibadan

OXFORD is a trade mark of Oxford University Press

Published in the United States
by Oxford University Press, New York

British Library Cataloguing in Publication Data
Colvin, H. M. (Howard Montagu), 1919–
All Souls: an Oxford college and its
buildings: the Chichele lectures: 1986.
1. Oxfordshire. Oxford. Universities:
Universities: University of Oxford.
Buildings. Architectural features
I. Title   II. Simmons, J. S. G. (John Simon
Gabriel)   III. Series
727'.3'0942574

ISBN 0–19–920161–7

Library of Congress Cataloging in Publication Data
Colvin, Howard Montagu.
All Souls, an Oxford College and its buildings: three lectures/
by Howard Colvin and J. S. G. Simmons.
(Chichele lectures: 1986)
Includes index.

1. All Souls College (University of Oxford)—Buildings—History.
2. All Souls College (University of Oxford)—Description—Views.
I. Simmons, John Simon Gabriel.   II. Title.   III. Series.
LF535.C65   1988   378.425'74—dc   19   88–23887

Set, printed and bound in Great Britain by
Butler & Tanner Ltd
Frome and London

PREFACE

THESE lectures were given in Hilary Term 1986 at the invitation of the Warden and Fellows of All Souls College and are now published more or less in the form in which they were delivered. The authors are grateful to the College for the honour of giving the lectures and for the opportunity to review three periods in its architectural history.

The first two chapters are concerned with the most important events in the history of the College buildings — the erection of the original quadrangle in the fifteenth century and the addition in the eighteenth century of the North Quadrangle and the Codrington Library to the designs of Nicholas Hawksmoor. The third chapter discusses the works carried out during the second half of the eighteenth and the first eighty years of the nineteenth century — a period of which no adequate account has hitherto been published. Appendix A contains the text of a chronicle of building activity in the College between the years 1553 and 1751. This in some degree fills the gap between chapters 1 and 2, besides recording the names of many benefactors to the College's building programmes. Appendix B is devoted to the text of Hawksmoor's letter to Dr George Clarke of 17 February 1714/15, which accompanied the drawings of his projected North Quadrangle. Appendix C prints a list of previous Chichele Lectures and is prefaced by a brief account of the inception of the series.

The best general sketch of the architectural history of All Souls is to be found in the section contributed by A. H. M. Jones to the third volume of the *Victoria County History of Oxfordshire*, published in 1954. This had been preceded by E. F. Jacob's study of the medieval building accounts which he contributed to *Essays Presented to James Tait* (Manchester, 1933). Any student of the architectural history of the College must acknowledge his debt to these two scholars, and so far as the medieval buildings are concerned, what they wrote calls for relatively little in the way of revision.

A formal architectural description of the earlier College buildings will be found in the volume on Oxford published in 1939 by the Royal Commission on Historical Monuments, but the accompanying plan is in some respects both inadequate and inaccurate, and a revised plan, incorporating changes subsequent to 1939, will be found at the end of this volume. The medieval glass in the Chapel was described by F. E. Hutchinson in *Medieval Glass at All Souls College* (1949) and the monumental inscriptions were the subject of a privately printed booklet by F. E. Hutchinson and Sir Edmund Craster entitled *Monumental Inscriptions in the Chapel of All Souls College, Oxford* (1949).

The authors are grateful to the Warden and Fellows of All Souls College, to the Provost and Fellows of Worcester College, to the Curators of the Bodleian Library, and to the authorities of the British Architectural Library of the RIBA and of Sir John Soane's Museum for generous permission to reproduce originals in their custody. They also wish to place on record their thanks to Dr Christopher Duggan of All Souls for supervising the production of the volume on behalf of the College.

H.M.C.
J.S.G.S.

May 1987

CONTENTS

List of Illustrations   viii

1   The Building of the Medieval College   I
    HOWARD COLVIN

2   Hawksmoor and the North Quadrangle   19
    HOWARD COLVIN

3   From Hawksmoor to Sir George Gilbert Scott   47
    J. S. G. SIMMONS

APPENDICES

A   Building at All Souls, 1553–1751: Selected Entries   78
    from the Warden's Register and the College Benefactors'
    Book
    HOWARD COLVIN

B   Hawksmoor's Letter to Dr George Clarke, dated   86
    17 February 1714/15
    HOWARD COLVIN

C   The Chichele Lectures, 1912–1988   91
    J. S. G. SIMMONS

Index   95

LIST OF ILLUSTRATIONS

Bird's-eye view of All Souls College in about 1600, known as the *Typus Collegii* — *Frontispiece*

1 The site of the College, showing the approximate boundaries of the properties as reconstructed by H. E. Salter — *Page* 3

2 Statue of Archbishop Chichele formerly standing in a niche in the front of the gate-tower — 7

3 David Loggan's engraved view of the College from the south, 1675 — 10

4 Block plan of the College before the eighteenth century — 10

5 Vault of vestibule between the Front Quadrangle and the medieval Hall — 11

6 The east side of the medieval Front Quadrangle with the Library on the upper floor — 12

7 The gate-tower from within the Front Quadrangle — 13

8 The gate-tower as seen from the High Street, 1816 — 14

9 Plan of medieval chambers showing the original arrangement of the studies — 15

10 The Front Quadrangle, looking towards the Chapel — 17

11 The High Street front of the Warden's Lodgings, as completed in 1706 — 21

12 Dr George Clarke's sketch-plan, c.1705 — 22

13 Design for the north side of the North Quadrangle by Dr George Clarke, c.1705–10 — 23

14 Design for the north side of the North Quadrangle attributed to Henry Aldrich, c.1705–10 — 24

15 Design for the north side of the North Quadrangle by William Townesend, dated 1709 — 25

16 Design for the north side of the North Quadrangle by John Talman, dated 1708 — 26

17 Design for the Hall and Chapel by John Talman, c.1708 — 26

18 Design for the north side of the North Quadrangle by Nicholas Hawksmoor — 27

19 Plan for the north side of the North Quadrangle by Nicholas Hawksmoor, with central corridor — 28

20 Another design for the north side of the North Quadrangle by Nicholas Hawksmoor — 28

21 Design for rebuilding the High Street front of the College in the classical style by Nicholas Hawksmoor — 29

22 Designs for rebuilding the High Street front of the College in the Gothic style by Nicholas Hawksmoor *Page* 29

23 Hawksmoor's plan of Feb. 1715 32

24 Perspective of the Codrington Library and North Quadrangle, as proposed by Nicholas Hawksmoor in Feb. 1715 34

25 Design by Nicholas Hawksmoor for the North Quadrangle, showing Gothic tracery in the windows of the Codrington Library 34

26 The centre of the Codrington Library, as seen from the passage between Hall and Chapel 35

27 Section of the Codrington Library as proposed by Hawksmoor, from an engraving dated 1717 35

28 Hawksmoor's Gothic towers, from Malton's *Views of Oxford*, 1802 36

29 Design for the Gothic towers by Hawksmoor made in 1715 37

30 The interior of the Hall, looking east 38

31 The interior of the Hall, looking west 39

32 The Cloisters, as seen from the North Quadrangle 40

33 The Buttery, showing the coffered ceiling and Hawksmoor's bust 40

34 The interior of the Cloisters, looking south 41

35 Perspective published in the *Oxford Almanack* for 1728 42

36 Design for the Gothic arcade across the Front Quadrangle, from an engraving dated 1721 43

37 Bust of Nicholas Hawksmoor at All Souls College by Sir Henry Cheere 45

38 Monument to Dr George Clarke in the Chapel 45

39 The east end of the Chapel, 1716–73 50

40 The east end of Magdalen College Chapel, 1817 51

41 *Noli me tangere*, painted by Raphael Mengs, 1769–71 53

42 The interior of the Codrington Library from the south east, 1802 53

43 High Street front: elevation before restoration, 1826 55

44 High Street front: unexecuted project for a regular Gothic restoration, 1826 55

45 Warden's Lodgings: unexecuted Gothic project for the High Street front, 1827 56

46 Warden's Lodgings: the Palladian High Street front as executed, 1827 57

47 The east end of the Chapel showing Dr George Clarke's panelling and pedimented central feature and Thornhill's fresco, 1817 59

48 The Chapel viewed from the east end showing Thornhill's screen (from Malton's aquatint of 1802–4) 60

49 The east end of New College Chapel showing Bernato Bernasconi's plaster reredos, 1803 61

50 The east end of Magdalen College Chapel showing the reredos, 1845 62

51 The east end of the Chapel as revealed in 1872   *Page* 64

52 The Chapel: Sir Gilbert Scott's drawing of the reredos, 1873   66

53 The Chapel: the east elevation of Sir Gilbert Scott's unexecuted
    project for a Gothic screen, 1875   67

54 The east end of the Chapel showing the reredos, as restored by Sir
    Gilbert Scott, with E. E. Geflowski's statuary, 1879   68

55 The east end of the Chapel, 1987, showing the Kempe retable of
    1889 over the altar   69

56 The credence in the north wall at the east end of the Chapel, 1876   71

57 The Chapel: unexecuted project for an outside stair, 1876   72

58 The south front of the Chapel showing Wren's sundial of 1659 in
    its original position, *c.*1870   73

59 A bird's-eye view of All Souls College from the south by E. H.
    New, 1923   76

60 Plan of the College in 1987   77

I

The Building of the Medieval College

WHEN Henry Chichele, Archbishop of Canterbury, founded All Souls College in 1438 it was at once an act of piety and an important educational initiative. What made it an act of piety was the obligation laid on the fellows daily to celebrate divine service not only for the souls of King Henry V, his brother Thomas, Duke of Clarence, and of the archbishop himself, but of all faithful departed, and in particular of those who, like the Duke of Clarence, had (in the archbishop's words) 'drunk the cup of bitter death' in the wars between England and France.[1]

Although Chichele was innocent of the pompous incitement to arms which Shakespeare (following Hall's Chronicle) puts into his mouth in the first act of *Henry V*, he must, as a leading royal councillor of that warlike monarch, be classed with the hawks rather than with the doves: so now, in his old age — he was in his seventies when he founded All Souls — he may well have felt some responsibility for the shedding of his countrymen's blood, however well justified Henry's claim to the French throne may have been. So his College was to be in some sort a Lancastrian war memorial, a place of remembrance for all those Englishmen who had lost their lives trying to turn a genealogical anomaly into a political reality.

But All Souls was also to serve a serious educational purpose. Conscious that the state of the clergy left much to be desired, both spiritually and intellectually, and observing that they had shared in the general demoralization that followed the English military failure in France, the archbishop established an academic society consisting of forty fellows, twenty-four of whom were to study arts, philosophy, or theology, and sixteen civil or canon law. All were to take Holy Orders, so that eventually they could go out into the world as members of that clerical *militia* whose decline the archbishop had observed with so much concern. Chichele's solicitude for the Church embraced the monastic as well as the secular clergy, and at the same time he was helping the Cistercians to establish St Bernard's College, a house of studies for members of their order in what is now St Giles'.[2]

---

[1] *Statutes of the Colleges of Oxford*, i (1853), All Souls, p. 11.

[2] For Chichele as archbishop, royal councillor, and founder of colleges, see E. F. Jacob's intro- duction to his edition of *The Register of Henry Chichele*, i (Canterbury and York Society, 1943); see also his *Archbishop Henry Chichele* (1967).

The combination of religious and academic functions represented by
Chichele's foundation was explicit or implicit in the constitutions of nearly
all the existing colleges of Oxford, but it was at New College that this kind
of foundation had been most fully developed. It was at New College that
Chichele himself had graduated as BCL in 1389, and it was to William of
Wykeham's statutes that he frequently turned as he drafted his own. As we
shall see, it was New College too that was to provide the architectural model
for All Souls.

The site chosen for Chichele's new college was in the heart of Oxford,
at the corner of High Street and Cat Street immediately east of St Mary's
Church. Its nucleus was an existing academic hall known as Barford or
Charlton's Hall, which Chichele was able to acquire in 1437. Oxford in the
early fifteenth century was a town in decline: many tenements were vacant
or falling into decay and the shops on the street-fronts concealed dereliction
behind. It was a situation which made it possible for colleges to be built in
formerly populous parts of the town in a manner which would have been out
of the question in the prosperous years of the twelfth and thirteenth centuries,
as it would be today. The result was that mix of university and urban property
which gives Oxford its special character, which prevented the emergence of
anything in the nature of a campus, and which of course made town and
gown partners — sometimes friendly and sometimes hostile — in a common
urban society.[3] (It may be added that to judge by their annual Christmas
present to those who in the esoteric Latinity of the College accounts were
called the *satraps* of the town, the fellows of All Souls in the fifteenth century
took pains to keep on good terms with the municipal authorities.)

So the foundation of All Souls at the corner of Cat Street and High Street
in 1438 formed part of the gradual take-over of a declining town by an
expanding university. It also formed part of the gradual replacement of
academic halls by colleges. In the thirteenth and fourteenth centuries only a
tiny minority of privileged fellows lived in colleges: many dons and most
students lived either in lodgings or in academic halls, which were the medieval
equivalents of what we should call hostels. But by the end of the sixteenth
century the newly founded colleges had not only taken over the functions of
the halls as places of residence, but had assumed responsibility for much of
the teaching that went on in the university. Of the former process All Souls
was a striking example: for according to the fifteenth-century antiquary John
Rouse, no fewer than six academic halls were destroyed to clear the site for

---

[3] For the economic decline of Oxford in the
later Middle Ages see H. E. Salter, *Medieval Oxford*
(Oxford Historical Society, 1936), pp. 87–9 and
Victoria County History of Oxfordshire, iv. 28–31.

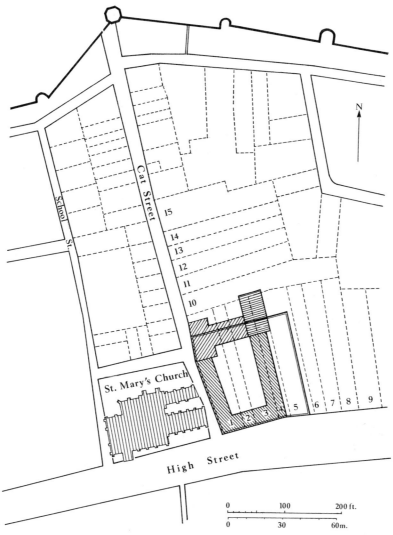

FIG. 1. The site of the College, showing the approximate boundaries of the properties as reconstructed by H. E. Salter. The double line represents the area 172 feet from north to south and 160 feet from east to west described as the site of the College in 1438. 1. Charlton's Inn. 2. Property of St Frideswide's Priory. 3. Property of St Mary's Church. 4. Property of Roger Skibbow. 5. Studley's Entry (property of Studley Priory). 6. Property formerly of Gilbert the Stationer. 7. Bedel Hall. 8. Barber's Court. 9. Ing Hall. 10. St Thomas Hall. 11. Grampound Hall. 12. Godknave Hall. 13. St John's Entry. 14. Tingewick Inn. 15. Mariole Hall.

Chichele's college.[4] Some but not all of them were identified by H. E. Salter in his map of medieval Oxford: Charlton's Inn, St Thomas Hall, and St John's Entry (Fig. 1).[5]

[4] A. Wood, *City of Oxford*, ed. A. Clark (Oxford Historical Society, 1889), i. 641.
[5] Salter, *Map of Medieval Oxford* (1934), map 3.

See also id., *Survey of Oxford*, ed. W. A. Pantin (Oxford Historical Society, 1960), i. 86–92, 127–35.

The acquisition of an adequate site for a new college was not, however, all that easy. Like a modern property developer, a founder might have to bide his time before he could get effective control of his chosen area. In the case of All Souls some of the owners were themselves corporate bodies whose legal right to dispose of their property required validation by higher authority. Chichele does not seem to have started the process early enough. The result was not only that the site was constricted, but building went ahead before all the freeholds were actually in his or the College's hands. At All Souls the most singular example of this was the Chapel, which stood on the site of St Thomas Hall. St Thomas Hall belonged to Oseney Abbey, yet it was not until May 1442, only a month before the first mass was said in the Chapel, that a licence was obtained for the monks of Oseney to alienate the hall to the College, and even then the College secured only a lease and not the freehold.[6] Incidentally, Salter's reconstruction of the boundaries of the properties on which the College was built cannot be quite accurate at this point, as the deeds relating to St Thomas Hall are explicit that it was the site of the Chapel:[7] evidently the southern boundary of the Hall should be drawn somewhat further south.

Figure 1 also shows the area 172 feet from north to south and 160 feet from east to west which is stated to be the site on which the College is to be built in a royal charter of confirmation dated May 1438.[8] This naturally does not include St Thomas Hall, but if Salter's map is correct it does include Studley's Entry, a property of Studley Priory of which the College seems to have acquired the lease, although it did not secure the freehold until after the dissolution of the priory in the 1530s.[9] However, the site of the College was clearly constricted in some way on the east side, for otherwise it is hard to understand why the quadrangle should be so narrow, or why the hall should have been so awkwardly placed at right-angles to the Chapel.

Despite the limitations, both physical and legal, of the site, work started on 10 February 1438, when a small party of the archbishop's men rode from Lambeth to Oxford to see the foundations laid. One of them was the surveyor of the works, a clerk named John Druell. He was a member of a family connected with the archbishop's own birthplace, Higham Ferrers in Northamptonshire, and was later to be archdeacon of Exeter. He must be distinguished from another man of the same name who was to become a fellow

[6] *The Oseney Cartulary*, ed. Salter (Oxford Historical Society, 1929), i. 194. For the earlier history of the property see id., *Survey*, i. 86–7.

[7] C. T. Martin, *Catalogue of the Archives in the Muniment Rooms of All Souls College* (1877), p. 154, no. 46. Hereafter documents in the College archives are cited by reference to the interleaved

copy of Martin in the Codrington Library at All Souls.

[8] *Calendar of Patent Rolls 1436–1441*, pp. 172–3, also printed in *Statutes of the Colleges of Oxford*, i (1853), All Souls, pp. 4–8.

[9] Salter, *Survey*, i. 132; Martin, *Catalogue*, p. 154.

of the College.[10] Druell was responsible for the general administration of the works, a task in which he was assisted by a clerk of works called John Medehill. The accounts kept by Medehill survive, and are the chief source of information about the building of All Souls.[11] They extend from 1438 to 1443. Some pages are lost at the end, but the main building operation is fully covered, and after Chichele's death in May 1443 the direction of the works must in any case have passed sooner or later from the archbishop's agents into the hands of the College.

The master mason throughout, and the man who must have been chiefly responsible for the design of the College, was called Richard Chevynton. Nothing is known of his previous career, and as he died in 1443 All Souls is his only recorded work. He had connections with Abingdon, and may well have been master mason to the abbey there.[12] His second-in-command, Robert Janyns, bore a name that was to be well-known in architectural circles later in the century, and was himself to be responsible for building the bell-tower of Merton College in the later 1440s.[13] At All Souls Janyns was for much of the time in charge on the site while Chevynton supervised the cutting of stone in the quarries at Burford. The walls were built mainly of stone from nearby Headington, where a quarry was leased for the purpose, but the superior freestone for windows, doorways, and other architectural components came from the Cotswold quarries near Burford and Taynton. It was the setting-out and correct cutting of the stones destined for these features that would have demanded Chevynton's expert attention, while Janyns saw to their laying at Oxford. Between them they had twenty to thirty masons at work building the new quadrangle after the existing houses and shops had been cleared away.

The chief carpenter was John Branche, who may, like Chevynton, have come from Abingdon, but the sculptor, John Massyngham, was a man of national standing from London.[14] As 4s. 8d. per week, plus board and lodging, he was more highly paid than either Chevynton or Branche, whose remuneration was 3s. 4d. a week, plus, in Chevynton's case, an annual retainer of £1. 6s. 8d.

Some 'great stone statues' over the high altar are specifically stated to have been Massyngham's work, and may have been the first instalment of the array of saints that was eventually to fill the niches that covered the windowless east wall of the Chapel. All these were of course destroyed at the Reformation and what we see today are Victorian replacements (Figs. 54–55).

[10] For the careers of the two John Druells see A. B. Emden, *Biographical Register of the University of Oxford to 1500*, i (1957), pp. 595–6.

[11] All Souls College MS CCCCI, hereafter cited as *Building Accounts*.

[12] J. Harvey, *English Mediaeval Architects* (1984), p. 52.

[13] Ibid., pp. 159–60.

[14] Ibid., pp. 32, 199–200; L. Stone, *Sculpture in Britain: the Middle Ages* (1955), pp. 206–9.

The figures of King Henry VI and Archbishop Chichele formerly in the niches on the front of the tower were also presumably Massyngham's work. The characterization of the young king and of the elderly archbishop is excellent, and if they are indeed Massyngham's work, reminds us that he was later to be involved in the making of the remarkably lifelike effigy of Richard Beauchamp at Warwick. However, these two statues, now preserved in the medieval cellar, have been cleaned and repaired on more than one occasion in the past, so their credentials as untouched specimens of fifteenth-century sculpture are not wholly satisfactory (Fig. 2).[15]

In the accounts some of the Taynton stone is specifically stated to have been for Massyngham's use, but other stone for making images was purchased at 'Rysborough', which must be the place of that name in Buckinghamshire. Risborough, on the edge of the Chilterns, was not a normal source of freestone, but there were quarries at Totternhoe, about sixteen miles away along the Icknield Way, and this may have been the source of the stone in question.

The timber was taken chiefly from nearby woods at Shotover, Stow Wood, Eynsham, Cumnor, and a place called Horeham — presumably the wood of that name near Marlow in Buckinghamshire which provided timber for the bell-tower of Merton College a few years later.[16] In 1438 ninety oaks were felled in Shotover and Stow Wood, and twenty more in Cumnor Wood, while the king gave twelve 'great oaks' from his park at Beckley. All this was hardwood, but the boards brought from Henley would probably have been of Baltic softwood shaped in London. The local timber was sawn up in a garden near the East Gate which was rented partly for this purpose and partly as a general depot for building materials for which there was no doubt insufficient space on the High Street site.

As was usual in medieval building operations, the work-force was paid by the day. Most of the workmen — masons, carpenters, joiners, sawyers, carvers, and so forth — were directly employed by the archbishop's agents, and little was done by contract or task-work. Such contracts as there were were mostly for specialized jobs such as making stained glass and patterned paving-tiles, but some slating was done by contract for £63, and when the completed quadrangle was paved in 1444, the work was done at the rate of 6d. a 'teese' or *toise* of seven square feet.[17] A paved quadrangle was an unusual refinement: indeed at the end of the seventeenth century it was remarked that

[15] In 1633 they were 'polished, smothed and renewed with vernishe, and guilt as formerly they had beene', and in 1826–7 they were 'repaired and cleaned' (*Victoria County History of Oxfordshire*, iii. 187).

[16] J. E. T. Rogers (ed.), *Oxford City Documents* (Oxford Historical Society, 1891), p. 327.

[17] For details of these tasks see E. F. Jacob, 'The Building of All Souls College, 1438–1443' in *Historical Essays in Honour of James Tait* (Manchester, 1933), p. 131.

FIG. 2. Statue of Archbishop Chichele formerly standing in a niche in the front of the gate-tower. *Thomas Photos*

All Souls was the only Oxford College whose quadrangle was entirely paved with stone.[18] This paving, now replaced by grass, can be seen in the Frontispiece.

Managing the workmen was a task which must have taken up a good deal of John Druell's time. The building-force needed frequent adjustment as the work progressed throughout different phases, and medieval building craftsmen were constantly coming and going of their own volition. In any one week, some would be employed for the whole week, some for five days, one or two perhaps for only two to three. Masons, in particular, were difficult to recruit and difficult to retain. If they came from a distance they were paid their travelling expenses and this is how we know that some of the All Souls masons came from London, from Norfolk and Suffolk, and from Fotheringhay in Northamptonshire. This was in the summer of 1441, the year of greatest activity, when the work-force reached a peak of over eighty, of whom about half were masons. But others were looking for masons too, and those in charge of the king's works could exercise the royal prerogative of impressment to secure them. Although Chichele had taken the precaution of obtaining a royal order exempting the workmen employed at All Souls from impressment, seven of the All Souls masons were nevertheless sent to Eton in September 1441 at the king's behest to work on his new college there.[19]

In the autumn of 1441 Druell retired from the surveyorship of the works at All Souls on his promotion to the wardenship of Maidstone College, a post in the archbishop's gift. His successor, Roger Keys, already a fellow of All Souls, was in 1443 to become its second Warden. Like his predecessor, he spent a good deal of time at the archbishop's palaces at Lambeth, Maidstone, and Croydon, taking delivery of money from Chichele's financial agents and rendering his own accounts there. Between them Druell and Keys spent about £3,894 on the archbishop's behalf between 1438 and 1443, but expenditure by other of Chichele's officials in connection with the works had brought the total to £4,156 by December 1442 and would have made it over £4,200 by the time of the archbishop's death in the following April.[20] This represented an average expenditure of £840 a year, or about one quarter of the archbishop's income from his landed estates, which was then somewhat over £3,000 per annum.[21] As he had held the see of Canterbury for over twenty years he may of course have had accumulated capital in hand. Unfortunately we do not have comparable figures for the building of any other medieval

[18] Bodleian Library MS Rawlinson D 810, fo. 25 (Oxford Historical Society, Collectanea, iv (1905), p. 200).
[19] H. Maxwell Lyte, History of Eton College (1911), pp. 11–13; Building Accounts, fo. 69.
[20] Building Accounts, fo. 97ᵛ.
[21] F. R. H. Du Boulay, The Lordship of Canterbury (1966), p. 244.

Oxford college, but both New College and Magdalen must have cost their respective founders a good deal more, and by the end of his reign Henry VI had contrived to spend nearly four times as much on building Eton College. But royal saints do not recognize the same constraints as ordinary mortals, and the £17,000 that Henry spent on Eton between 1441 and 1461 included half-building the chapel and then pulling it down because he did not like the first design.[22]

What were the architectural results of this outlay? There can be no doubt that, in Chichele's eyes, as later in Waynflete's, New College was the model to follow in planning his own foundation. At New College, hall and chapel formed an imposing block on the north side of a residential quadrangle entered from the west through a gate-tower which formed part of the Warden's lodging. There was a library in the eastern range of the quadrangle and beyond the chapel there was a cloister and a detached bell-tower. Whether or not the T-shaped chapel with its truncated nave was the result of accident or design, it apparently provided a sufficiency of altars for collegiate purposes, and Chichele copied it at All Souls. Though considerably smaller than its prototype, All Souls Chapel, with its hammer-beam roof, its tiers of saints at the east end, its carved stalls, its stained glass and its figured paving-tiles, was no less highly ornamented. What is more its forty-two stalls could accommodate all its forty fellows, whereas at New College there were only sixty-two stalls for a complement of seventy fellows. Besides the high altar there were six altars in the nave or antechapel, four against the east wall, and two against the screen; and there was another in the vestry which formerly projected from the north side of the choir.[23]

The Chapel occupied the whole width of the narrow quadrangle (Fig. 3): although it would probably have been physically possible to build the Hall on the same alignment, as at New College, it was decided to site it at right-angles to the Chapel (Fig. 4). The reasons for this odd arrangement are no longer fully apparent, but given that the east range of the quadrangle could not be sited further east, the relationship between Hall and quadrangle was bound to be more or less awkward. Access to the Hall from the quadrangle was by means of a fan-vaulted vestibule in the north-east corner of the latter (Fig. 5), and the buttery cellar was tucked in under the east end of the Chapel. All Souls must have been the only religious establishment in England where the beer was kept immediately underneath the high altar. The medieval Hall was of course demolished in 1730, and all that we know of its appearance is derived from the bird's-eye view in the *Typus Collegii* of about 1600, in

---

[22] H. M. Colvin (ed.), *History of the King's Works*, i (1963), pp. 284–92.
[23] *Victoria County History of Oxfordshire*, iii. 184.

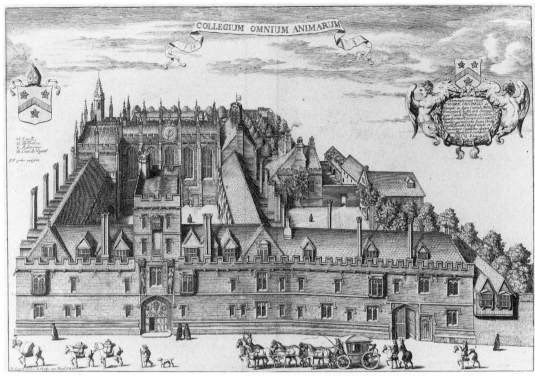

FIG. 3 David Loggan's engraved view of the College from the south, 1675. *Ashmolean Museum, Oxford*

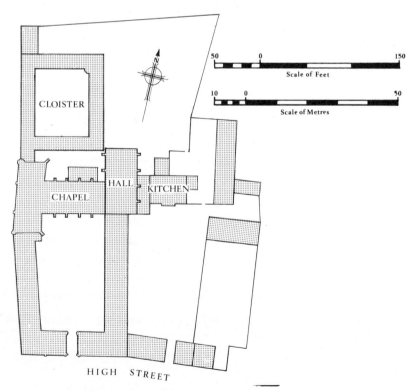

FIG. 4. Block plan of the College before the eighteenth century

FIG. 5. Vault of vestibule between the Front Quadrangle and the medieval Hall

which its buttresses, traceried windows, and louver[24] can just be discerned (Frontispiece). The kitchen stood immediately to the east. The Library (Fig. 6) occupied part of the upper floor of the east range of the quadrangle, as at New College, and there are payments in the accounts to joiners making the 'deskes' for the accommodation of the books.[25] Its structure still survives, but the plaster ceiling dates from 1598, and the Georgian Gothic panelling recalls its conversion into a set of rooms in 1751. The placing of the gateway in the southern rather than the western range of the quadrangle represents a minor divergence from the New College model, but one that is readily under- standable as it gave the College access to the High Street rather than to a narrow side-street. The gatehouse itself was one of a standard Oxford type developed from the one at New College, consisting of a mere prolongation upwards of the walls above the two archways, without external or internal projection (Figs. 7, 8). This modest treatment of the gateway, whose expression as a separate architectural structure is still further compromised by running

[24] The louver seen in the view is presum- ably the one built in 1501/2 by Robert Carowe, master carpenter (Martin, *Catalogue*, p. 405, *computus* 1501/2).

[25] *Building Accounts*, fos. 41ᵛ, 51 ('le joyneres operantibus circa le deskes in libraria factis').

FIG. 6. The east side of the medieval Front Quadrangle with the Library on the upper floor

the main string-course straight across it, is one of several features which distinguish Oxford collegiate architecture from that of Cambridge. In general one may say that basically the Cambridge college is an academic version of a later medieval manor-house, of which the gatehouse is often a prominent feature, whereas the Oxford college was (from New College onwards) a single architectural entity in which the gatehouse was a subordinate feature. It may be significant that several Cambridge colleges had secular founders, whereas most pre-Reformation Oxford colleges owed their existence to bishops who were naturally disposed to follow the precedent established by one of their own order. At any rate the adoption, at both the colleges built under Chichele's aegis, St Bernard's and All Souls, of this basic type of gatehouse, provided a formula that was to be followed later at Balliol, Merton, and Corpus, though not at Magdalen, Brasenose or Christ Church.

Finally, the living accommodation followed closely the New College pattern of a shared chamber with three or four studies partitioned off in the corners (Fig. 9). It was of course this arrangement that produced the alternation of two-light and single-light windows that can still be seen in the quadrangle (Figs. 6, 7). On this basis the College could accommodate some sixty fellows or students, but this was more than the statutory complement of forty,

FIG. 7. The gate-tower from within the Front Quadrangle

and it was subsequently decided by John Stafford, Chichele's successor as Archbishop of Canterbury and Visitor of the College, that the eight senior fellows should share eight of the first-floor rooms with only one companion each, while the remaining twenty-four fellows were to be disposed by threes in eight other chambers. The five remaining chambers were to be occupied by the chaplains, clerks, choristers, and servants. The Warden enjoyed the use of the rooms on the first floor immediately to the east of the tower.[26]

[26] *Statutes of the Colleges of Oxford*, i (1853), All Souls, pp. 72–3; *Victoria County History of Oxfordshire*, iii. 187.

FIG. 8. The gate-tower as seen from the High Street. Mackenzie and Pugin, *Specimens of Gothic Architecture* (1816)

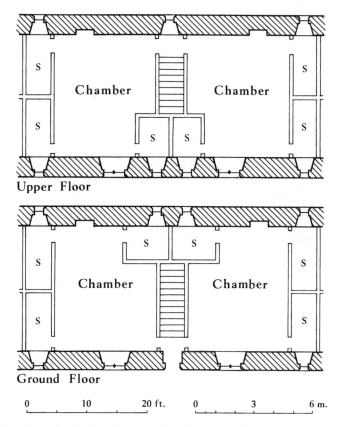

FIG. 9. Plan of medieval chambers showing the original arrangement of the studies
(marked S)

Two components of the New College model remained to be built: a cloister and a bell-tower. For these a site was obtained by the acquisition of further tenements on the east side of Cat Street to the north of the Chapel. All these tenements up to and including Tingewick's Inn were in the hands of the College by 1449 at the latest, but the fellows were not yet in a position to embark on another major building operation at their own expense, and it was not until 1460 that any move was made to develop the site. On 13 August of that year a suffragan bishop consecrated what is variously described as 'the cemetery', 'the cloister', or 'the place where the cloister is to be built'.[27] Little progress, however, appears to have been made until the latter part of the fifteenth century, but by 1491 three sides of the cloister had been constructed. In that year the College appealed to various well-beneficed friends for funds to complete it by building the fourth side. As the function of a cloister in collegiate life is not immediately obvious, it may be worth adding that

[27] Martin, *Catalogue*, p. 405, *computus* for 1459–60, various payments, e.g. for gloves 'dat' episcopo quando consecravit claustrum'; 3s. 4d. given 'famulis Suffragan' consecrantis cemeterium'; 4s. 4d. paid to labourers 'circa mundacionem ubi claustrum debet situari'.

[28] All Souls College, Warden's MS 1, fos. 35–6, 49.

according to one of these letters the All Souls cloister was used for processions, for private prayer, and for burials.[28] It seems to have been finished soon afterwards, with the aid of contributions from James Goldwell, Bishop of Norwich, and others.[29] Its form is shown in the *Typus*, and a good deal of what was probably its blank west wall remains incorporated in the existing Georgian cloister (Fig. 34).

The bell-tower of course was never built, but when, in 1571–2, four chambers were constructed on a vacant space immediately to the north of the cloister, it was remembered that this was the site where it was, 'as is said, purposed to builde a steeple uppon at the beginning'.[30] Had a tower been built on this site, particularly if it was a large ornamental one like Magdalen Tower, the development of the north quadrangle in the eighteenth century might have taken a very different form.

In style the new College was what is called 'Perpendicular' — that is the Gothic peculiar to fifteenth-century England in which rectilinear rather than curvilinear forms are predominant. We can see this clearly in the gate-tower, in the square-headed frames to the doorways, and in the tracery of the Chapel windows (Fig. 10). New College had been an early and rather austere example of this style, but since the 1390s there had been a tendency to develop a more elaborate and decorative form of Perpendicular, characterized by complex mouldings and other enrichments. This in its turn yielded to a simpler version of the style which became fashionable in the 1440s. In Oxford the change in taste is documented by the letter of 1440 in which the university authorities instructed their master mason, Thomas Elkyn, to abandon what they called the 'superfluous elaboration' of the work so far executed in the new Divinity School and to continue in a simpler style.[31] The result can still be seen in the jambs of the windows, where the earlier mouldings are cut off short by the simplified ones of the 1440s. In the revised instructions which Henry VI gave for building Eton College Chapel in 1448 he too expressed disapproval of 'superfluity of too great curious works of entail (i.e. carving) and busy moulding'.[32] At All Souls (as at St Bernard's College, then being built by the Cistercians with Chichele's help) the mouldings are relatively plain and the chapel windows conform to the new 'gridiron' type in which the mullions run straight from sill to soffit of the arch and the tracery is of simplified character. The effect is by no means unhandsome, but if one compares the choir of All Souls with the chancel of Adderbury Church, built by the original

[29] Entry in sixteenth-century College Register under 1491: 'Hoc circiter tempus collegii claustra aedificantur impensis partim collegii partim Jacobi Goldwel episcopi Norvic. Mri. Thomae Colfoxe et aliorum'.

[30] All Souls College, Warden's MS 3, fo. 12.
[31] H. Anstey (ed.), *Epistolae Academicae Oxon.* (Oxford Historical Society, 1898), p. 192.
[32] Colvin, *King's Works*, i. 288.

Fig. 10. The Front Quadrangle, looking towards the Chapel

master mason of the Divinity School in the second decade of the fifteenth century, one can see how the decorative style of Henry V's reign has been modified. Only in the gate-tower was there any external display and this was achieved by means of the large canopied niches containing statues of Henry VI and the Founder and above them Christ in Judgement (Fig. 8).

How far the important architectural decisions were taken by Chichele himself, or by Druell and Keys, or by the master mason, we do not know. No drawing, specification, or archiepiscopal direction survives to give us any information about the genesis of the design, nor are there any payments (such as are sometimes found in medieval building records) for parchment upon which to make 'patrons' or drawings. Unlike William of Wykeham, Chichele had not been a clerk of the royal works, so he may not have had quite the same practical experience of architectural affairs. So far as we know, his only visit to inspect his new College was when he come to consecrate the Chapel in June 1442.[33] His health was already failing and in the fifteenth century the journey from Lambeth to Oxford was not one to be undertaken lightly by an ailing man in his late seventies. But the frequent visits of his agents to his palaces at Lambeth, Otford, Croydon, or Maidstone would have kept him in touch with the progress of the works. On one occasion in 1438/9 Druell took with him both the master mason and the master carpenter, which suggests that features of the design were being discussed.[34] It was fortunate that the aged archbishop survived long enough to see his College completed in its

---

[33] Wood, *History of the Colleges and Halls*, ed. J. Gutch (1786), pp. 287–8 n.
[34] *Building Accounts*, fo. 18.

essentials and established as a corporate body. The death in 1421 of Richard
Clifford, Bishop of London, had meant the end of his embryonic London
College, and if Chichele had died a year or two earlier All Souls might have
found itself in difficulties. As it was Chichele survived just long enough to
give the College the authorized copy of its statutes on 2 April 1443: and when
he died ten days later he would have known that his foundation was virtually
complete and that he had done all that lay in his power to ensure the
continuance, *pro perpetuis futuris temporibus*, of the college of poor scholars
commonly called 'All Soulen College'.[35]

[35] *Statutes of the Colleges of Oxford*, i (1853), All Souls, p. 11.

2

Hawksmoor and the North Quadrangle

HOWEVER far removed in spirit and achievement from the academic ideals either of the fifteenth or of the twentieth century, All Souls College did in the first half of the eighteenth century distinguish itself by the erection of buildings that are perhaps more admired today than those of the Founder himself. Architectural activity is no guarantee of academic standards: and the All Souls which give Hawksmoor one of his greatest commissions was a factious club of largely absentee fellows frequently at odds with their Warden.[1] It is surprising that a mutinous and politically divided College should have successfully carried out a major building programme. But fellows whose behaviour so often vexed their Warden, worried their Visitor, and contravened both the letter and the spirit of their Statutes were, it seems, united in wishing to see their College gloriously rebuilt. To this end they were prepared to forgo gaudies, to dun their wealthy friends and relations, to contribute often generously out of their own pockets, and to endure for years on end the noise and inconvenience of building.

In this the fellows of All Souls were not of course unique. The early eighteenth century was a period of great architectural activity in Oxford, when the Clarendon Building was erected and the Radcliffe Library was planned, and when several colleges were wholly or largely rebuilt: and not only in Oxford — for this was a time when a Tory government provided funds with which to carry out an ambitious programme of church-building in London, when Blenheim and Castle Howard were under construction, and many lesser country houses were being built or rebuilt. In fact the second decade of the eighteenth century marks one of the great building booms in English history, and the Tory government and the gentry were its principal promoters.

All Souls in the early eighteenth century was both predominantly Tory in its political sympathies and aristocratic in its social connections. In 1852 the University Commissioners observed that at All Souls 'birth and general social qualifications' had been influential in the election of Wardens as far back as

---

[1] For the College in the eighteenth century see M. Burrows, *The Worthies of All Souls* (1874), chaps. 19–22 and E. F. Jacob in *Victoria Country History of Oxfordshire*, iii. 179–80.

the 1680s, and in those of fellows 'at least as far as the commencement of the present century'. They might, as Montagu Burrows remarked, have gone even further back in the case of fellows.[2] In the first quarter of the eighteenth century All Souls already had that strongly upper-class character that was to persist into the middle of the nineteenth. When the hostile Hearne declared in 1714 that most of the fellows of All Souls were 'persons of great fortunes and high birth and of little morals and less learning',[3] he was giving vent to his prejudices, but conveying an element of truth. So it was natural that the fellows of an aristocratic college should share the tastes of their class and want to participate in the architectural activity that they saw wherever they went. What is more, the wealth of some of them, and the social and family connections of others, were to ensure that money would be forthcoming for the building programme. The new buildings at All Souls were not built out of corporate revenue, but by bequest, gift, loan, and subscription on the part of fellows, quondam fellows, and their friends.

Elsewhere in Oxford new buildings such as Peckwater Quadrangle at Christ Church and the new range overlooking the park at Magdalen were designed for the accommodation of gentlemen commoners, a relatively new class of undergraduates who were able and willing to pay for superior accommodation. Then, as now, All Souls admitted no commoners, but its fellows were gentlemen to a man, and they must have found the medieval shared rooms quite unfitted for their style of life. So in the course of time the chambers in the Old Quadrangle were rearranged to accommodate one fellow each where the Founder had provided for two or three. But this meant that there would no longer be room for all the resident fellows, so a new building was needed.

In 1703 Dr George Clarke took the initiative by offering to build lodgings in the College at his own expense: they were to be his for life and thereafter to revert to the College as a residence for its Warden.[4] Dr Clarke was then a man in his forties, a fellow of over twenty years' standing, and a Tory politician. A lawyer by training, he had been appointed Judge-Advocate General by Charles II and Secretary at War by William III, and had recently become Secretary to the Queen's husband, Prince George of Denmark, and Joint Secretary of the Admiralty. He was an able and enlightened man who combined immense experience of public affairs with a deep interest in the arts and above all in that of architecture. He was building up a magnificent architectural library, and he was something of an architect himself. His own drawings were amateurish in technique, but they were quite sufficient to

[2] Burrows, *Worthies*, pp. 247–8.
[3] D. W. Rannie (ed.), *Hearne's Collections*, iv

(Oxford Historical Society, 1898), p. 333.
[4] *Victoria County History of Oxfordshire*, iii. 190.

FIG. 11. The High Street front of the Warden's Lodgings, as completed in 1706.
W. Williams, *Oxonia Depicta* (1732–3)

enable him to work out architectural schemes which could subsequently be elaborated by others. He was one of the Commissioners for building the new churches in London and he knew all the leading English architects of his day. In Oxford he had a hand in every major building project from the Clarendon Building to Worcester College, and at All Souls he was the guiding spirit behind all the new schemes of the early eighteenth century.[5]

In 1703 the only sites available for expansion were to the north, where the medieval cloister and the tenements beyond as far as the site of Hertford College were now either owned or leased by All Souls, and along the High Street immediately to the east, where an adjoining house had recently been purchased by the College. Clarke's first intention was to build on the northern site, and with this in view the College in 1703 demolished the old cloisters and built a new colonnade of paired Ionic columns along the Cat Street frontage north of the Chapel. This was to link any new building to the Old Quadrangle. Who designed this colonnade we do not know, but the capitals of the Ionic Order were taken from Scamozzi, a standard seventeenth-century architectural textbook. Examples of them can still be seen re-used in the passage between the two quadrangles and in the Hall screen.[6]

[5] For Clarke see *Dictionary of National Biography* and H.M. Colvin, *A Biographical Dictionary of British Architects 1600–1840* (1978). For the architectural drawings in his collection, now in Worcester College Library, see Colvin, *A Catalogue of Architectural Drawings of the Eighteenth and Nineteenth Centuries in the Library of Worcester College, Oxford* (1964) and J. Harris and A. A. Tait, *Catalogue of the Drawings of Inigo Jones, John Webb and Isaac de Caus at Worcester College, Oxford* (1979).

[6] The demolition of the cloister is recorded in All Souls College, Warden's MS 3, fo. 79. A drawing in Worcester College Library (no. 38) notes that 'the Capitall is after Scamozzi'. For the subsequent re-use of the columns from the cloister see Martin, *Catalogue*, pp. 294–5, nos. 42, 44, 45, 47, 52.

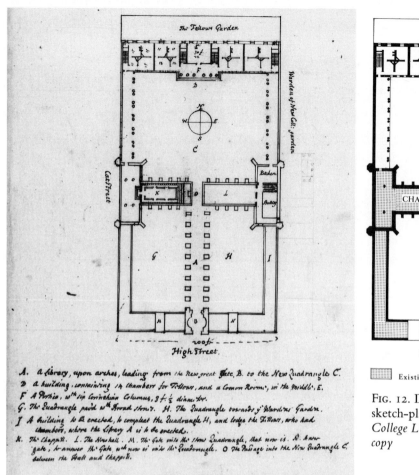

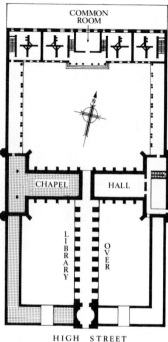

A. *a Library, upon arches, leading from the New great Gate B. to the New Quadrangle C.*
D. *a building containing 14 chambers for Fellows, and a Common Roome, in the middle, E.*
F. *A Portico, with six Corinthian Columns, 3 ft ½ diameter.*
G. *The Quadrangle paved with Broad stone. H. The Quadrangle towards ye Warden's Garden.*
I. *A building to be erected, to compleat the Quadrangle H, and lodge the Fellows, who had chambers, where the Library A is to be erected.*
K. *The Chappell. L. The New hall. M. The Gate into the Stone Quadrangle, that now is. N. A new gate, to answer the Gate which now is into the Quadrangle. O. The Passage into the New Quadrangle C. between the Hall and Chappell.*

Existing buildings retained.

FIG. 12. Dr George Clarke's sketch-plan, c. 1705. *Worcester College Library, with a modern copy*

However, Clarke changed his mind and instead built on the High Street front the house that is now the Warden's lodgings. This was completed in April 1706.[7] It had a regular front of a straightforward kind, battlemented to indicate its status as part of the College (Fig. 11). This left the northern site vacant, and the College determined to pursue the idea of building there. Dr Clarke, who since 1705 had been out of office following a change of government, took the architectural initiative, and produced a sketch-plan which was to be the basis of all the schemes that followed (Fig. 12).

What it adumbrated was far more than just providing a new residential range: with the exception of the Chapel, the south and west ranges of the Old Quadrangle, and the newly built colonnade, the entire College was to be rebuilt. The awkward relationship of the Hall to the rest of the College was to be remedied by rebuilding it in line with the Chapel, on the New College model. The buttery and kitchen were to be rehoused in a block at the east end of the Hall that would externally mirror the antechapel. A much enlarged

[7] All Souls College, Warden's MS 3, fo. 80.

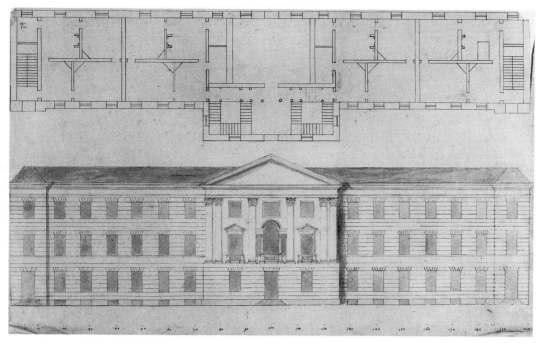

FIG. 13. Design for the north side of the North Quadrangle by Dr George Clarke, c. 1705–10.
Worcester College Library

Old Quadrangle was to be divided in two by a Library standing on arches on
the site of the existing east range. As later at Worcester College this arcade
with the Library above it was to provide covered circulation from the main
entrance to Hall and Chapel. To the north there was to be a completely new
quadrangle with a large new building on the north side linked to the Chapel
by the existing colonnade on the west and to the rebuilt Hall by a matching
colonnade on the east.

The residential building on the north side of the new North Quadrangle
was obviously the first priority. It was designed to house fourteen fellows in
spacious sets of four rooms each, and in the centre, behind the portico, was
to be the Common Room. The Common Room was the social centre of the
College, and throughout all the schemes that followed, it retained its central
position. In most Oxford colleges the Senior Common Room is unobtrusively
situated, but at All Souls it is still the focal point of the North Quadrangle,
though not in the position envisaged by Dr Clarke in 1705.

During the next four years several architects were invited by Dr Clarke to
submit plans and elevations for a building on the lines he had laid down.[8]
Clarke himself made two sketches, one for a building with a façade articulated
by a giant order, another with one of Palladian character based on a drawing
by the seventeenth-century architect John Webb that he had in his own

[8] All these drawings are now in Worcester College Library and are listed in my *Catalogue* (see
n. 5, above).

FIG. 14. Design for the north side of the North Quadrangle attributed to Henry Aldrich, *c.* 1705–10. *Worcester College Library*

collection (Fig. 13). These two drawings are characteristic specimens of Clarke's inelegant but serviceable draughtsmanship. Much more accomplished is a drawing provided by his friend Dean Aldrich of Christ Church (Fig. 14).[9] The plan is virtually identical, but the elevation is dominated by a great hexastyle Corinthian portico conceived as a temple-front embedded in the building. It was with just such a portico that, some ten years later, Colen Campbell was to embellish one of the key buildings of the Palladian revival, Wanstead House in Essex, and Aldrich's All Souls design emphasizes his status as an academic forerunner of English Palladianism. All the other designs bespoken by Dr Clarke, from the London master carpenter Edward Wilcox, the Oxford master mason William Townesend (Fig. 15), or the connoisseur architect John Talman, were more or less baroque in character. Talman's, as might be expected of an architect who had spent much of his life in France, Germany, and Italy, were very different from the insular baroque of Wilcox or Townesend. With its oval staircase-projection, its flattened dome, and its jaunty pediments, his elevation (dated 1708) recalls the baroque of Southern Europe, and, more specifically, the work of Guarino Guarini at Turin. His plan is instructive, for it designates the rooms comprising each set as 'Outward Room, Entertaining Room, Library, Bed Chamber', and 'Closet' (Fig. 16).

At the same time Talman produced some remarkable designs for remodelling the Chapel and rebuilding the Hall, in a North Italian Gothic style (Fig. 17). Their northern elevations were to be bedecked with statuary and panels of coloured ornament. In the middle, on a central buttress, there was to be a bronze statue of the Founder, *in pontificalibus*, flanked on either side by two 'Romish bishops' wearing mitres and two 'Reformed Bishops' wearing Geneva caps, thus symbolizing the pre- and post-Reformation history of the

[9] When these were first published in 1964 they were ascribed to John James, but comparison with drawings by Aldrich makes it clear that nos. 12 and 39 and probably also nos. 30 and 31 are by him, and that no. 14, though in James's hand, is a fair copy of Aldrich's design.

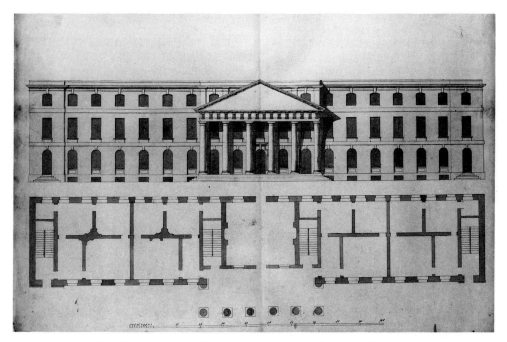

FIG. 15. Design for the north side of the North Quadrangle by William Townesend, dated 1709. *Worcester College Library*

College. Below them statues of benefactors 'in brass' were to stand against the wall between each pair of buttresses, and above them the parapet was to be studded with finials of gilded metal. The result, as he said, would be 'unlike any other in Oxford and pretty much after the Italian Gothick, which I hope will be no disparagement'. The interior of the Hall was likewise to be Italianized, with 'grotesche' painted on the vault, and a great baroque painting on the south wall (blocking the windows) showing Apollo surrounded by the Muses distributing prizes to 'multitudes of students in their proper habits (whose faces are to be from the life)'. At one end there would be a painted representation of King Henry VI confirming the foundation of the College, and at the other a screen with a central niche for the display of the College plate 'on solemn days'.[10] Despite the attractions of Talman's elegantly coloured drawings, it is not likely that this exotic scheme was ever seriously entertained by Dr Clarke and his colleagues.

Finally there was Nicholas Hawksmoor, who submitted as many schemes of his own as all the other architects put together, and who was eventually to rebuild the quadrangle, though not in accordance with his first designs. For these were as unrealistic in their way as Talman's — they were visionary dreams of baroque grandeur far beyond the College's likely resources, but each a masterpiece of the architectural drama that we can experience in his

[10] For coloured reproductions of these drawings see my *Unbuilt Oxford* (1983), pl. 1.

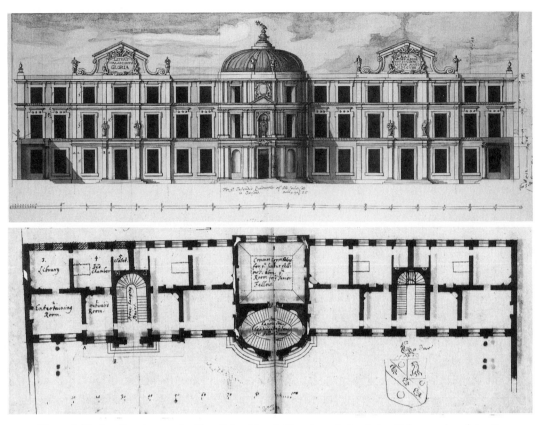

FIG. 16. Design for the north side of the North Quadrangle by John Talman, dated 1708.
Worcester College Library

FIG. 17. Design for the Hall and Chapel by John Talman, *c.* 1708. *Worcester College Library*

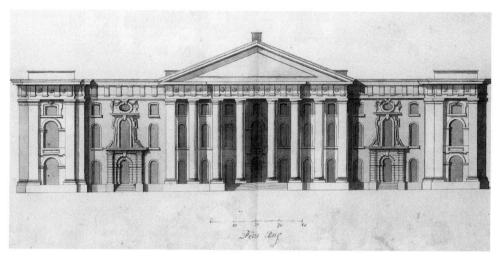

FIG. 18. Design for the north side of the North Quadrangle by Nicholas Hawksmoor.
Worcester College Library

London churches or in the palace at Woodstock that he helped Vanbrugh to realize. Figure 18 shows a version with a great Doric portico engrossing nearly half the façade beneath a wide-spreading pediment; Figure 19 a variant plan with a spinal corridor, a new idea in Oxford collegiate architecture no doubt suggested by the one Vanbrugh had recently designed at Blenheim. In this, as in some other schemes, the pediment was to be subordinated to an arched attic feature which would have given All Souls, like Blenheim, a picturesque skyline composed of strictly classical elements (Fig. 20). At the same time Hawksmoor produced designs for a new High Street front of equal grandeur, its centre-piece a triumphal archway surmounted by a circular domed tempietto (Fig. 21). But in practice it was likely that the south and west sides of the Old Quadrangle would be retained, as indeed Dr Clarke had envisaged in his plan, so Hawksmoor produced an alternative front in the Gothic style with the existing entrance tower retained (though remodelled) and duplicated (for the sake of symmetry) on the other side of the new and loftier central one (Fig. 22).

There was little hope that any of these grandiose schemes would be realized. In 1709 Townesend submitted estimates which indicated that it would cost £1,075 to build the Common Room 'after the designe with the Corinthian pillars', and £1,262 more to rebuild the Hall and kitchen to correspond to the Chapel.[11] But the corporate revenue had no surplus for such purposes, and so far no benefactor had come forward.

Then in 1710 came the news of a spectacular bequest. Christopher Codrington, a quondam fellow who owned vast estates in the West Indies, died unmarried, leaving the College £10,000 (£6,000 to build a library and £4,000

[11] Martin, *Catalogue*, p. 291, no. 8b(1).

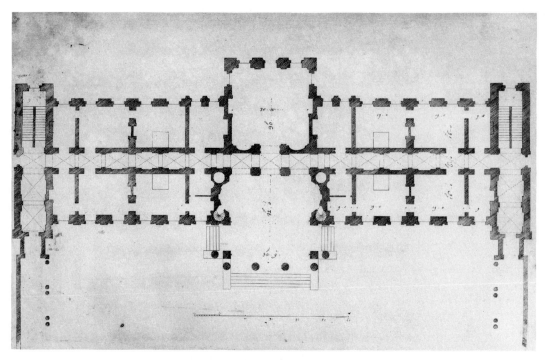

FIG. 19. Plan for the north side of the North Quadrangle by Nicholas Hawksmoor, with central corridor. *Worcester College Library*

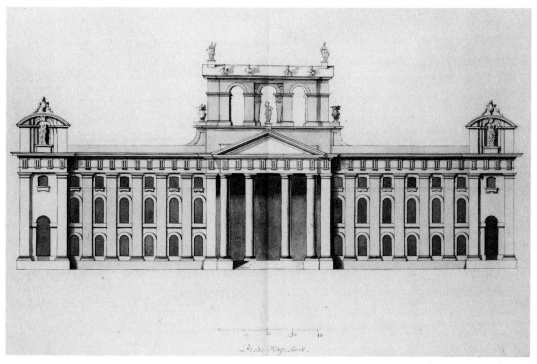

FIG. 20. Another design for the north side of the North Quadrangle by Nicholas Hawksmoor. *Worcester College Library*

FIG. 21. Design for rebuilding the High Street front of the College in the classical style by Nicholas Hawksmoor. *Worcester College Library*

FIG. 22. Design for rebuilding the High Street front of the College in the Gothic style by Nicholas Hawksmoor. *Worcester College Library*

to buy books). This eventually resulted in a reconsideration of the whole
design. The Library was now to take the place of the Common Room and
'Grand Dormitory' as the key building in the projected North Quadrangle.
It would occupy the north side of what was now envisaged as a three-
sided quadrangle with the fellows' sets on the east side. This had important
architectural consequences. It changed the main axis from north–south to
east–west. Now the new Library would answer to the Chapel and rebuilt
Hall. What is more it brought the new North Quadrangle into relationship
with another exciting new development that was soon to be very much in
Clarke's and Hawksmoor's minds — the creation of the Radcliffe Square.
Instead of running alongside a narrow street the new quadrangle would face
a formal square containing a monumental building, designed if all went well
by Hawksmoor himself. Both the building of the Library and the clearance
of the square had to wait for the lawyers to do their work in winding up the
estates of the two benefactors — Codrington and Radcliffe — and securing
the title to the land to be built on. So there was ample time in which to
prepare new designs, and these when they came proved to be in the Gothic
style.

The logic of this change from classic to Gothic is easy to understand. If the
new Library was to balance the Hall and Chapel on the north side of the new
quadrangle, then it must correspond in style: so compelling was the idea of
symmetry to eighteenth-century architectural minds that the Library even
had to have a western appendage like the antechapel and an identical façade
to the new square (Fig. 24). In a situation where a medieval architect would
at most have aimed at a rough balance, an eighteenth-century Gothicist felt
impelled to impose a strict and quite unmedieval symmetry on his plan. In
fact I think one can say that the choice of the Gothic style itself was due less
to any sentimental or antiquarian preference than to the compulsion of
symmetry about the new east–west axis.

The complete scheme, as Hawksmoor envisaged it in February 1715, was
illustrated by a set of six large drawings accompanied by a written 'Explanation'. Of these six drawings only three survive: the plan (Fig. 23) and two
others which will be mentioned later.[12] On this plan the Old Quadrangle is
shown in broken lines, and in his 'Explanation' Hawksmoor asks 'leave to say
something in favour of the Old Quadrangle, built by your most Revd.
Founder', which he said was 'strong and durable' and deserved careful treat-

---

[12] The 'Explanation' was published by the
College in 1960 with a portfolio of the engravings
of 1717 and 1721, which incorporate subsequent
modifications. One of the three surviving drawings of 1715 ('No. 1') is now at Worcester College
(no. 70), the other two being in the Bodleian
Library (MS Gough Plans 7 = 'No. 6' and MS
Gough Plans 8 = 'No. 2').

ment if it was to be retained. Hawksmoor's concern here was not the preservation of the Old Quadrangle as an unaltered specimen of fifteenth-century
collegiate architecture, but its adaptation in a manner that would not destroy
its architectural character. He particularly warns the College against allowing
the outward mouldings on the jambs of the windows to be cut away, 'for
that' (as he rightly says) 'takes off all the ornament and strength of the design'.
But he envisaged adding an upper storey carefully designed both to preserve
a reasonable regularity and to 'strike in with those small irregularities frequent
in the Gothick works', and as a later perspective shows, he was quite prepared
to pull it down and start afresh if the College wished (Fig. 35). Hawksmoor
was not a conservationist before his time, but as an architect concerned with
ancient buildings he did rightly deplore their thoughtless and barbarous
mutilation in a manner that was all too common in the eighteenth century.

On 19 February 1715 the College agreed 'that the Library ... should be
built as the College Chappell was, according to the model [i.e. design] that
was then shown to the Society, and that Dr. Clarke and Sir Nathaniel Lloyd
be desired to be inspectors, and take care of the sayd buildings.'[13] The contract
with Townesend was signed in 1716,[14] and on 21 June the foundation was
laid of what the inscription grandiloquently called the 'Bibliotheca Chichleio-
Codringtoniana'.[15] It was in several respects an unusual building for a library.
Large libraries of that period were almost invariably on the first floor, to
protect the contents against damp, but here the need to match the Chapel
made that impossible, and a cellar effectively performed the same function.
The idea of entering the Library in the middle, inherited from the residential
building, was also a novelty, and rather an awkward one, as no vestibule was
envisaged inside. Later generations have not surprisingly made the western
entrance the principal one and the oval lawn (formed in 1765) has played
down the subsidiary north–south axis, which in 1716 was still very much in
the minds of the College and its architect.

Internally the Library as built deviates considerably from Hawkmoor's
intentions. The 'Explanation' of 1715 shows that he envisaged a vista of Gothic
arches, which are shown on the plan (Fig. 23). Those in the centre were to
support a turret 'with windows striking down into the room' and arranged
'in the form of a Gothick lantern'. The exterior of this lantern can be seen in
Figure 24, and there was to be a corresponding lantern over the passage

---

[13] *Victoria County History of Oxfordshire*, iii. 191.
[14] Ibid.
[15] Bodleian Library, MS Rawlinson D 1054,
fo. 82, giving the inscription on the foundation
stone. The text is printed in A. Wood, *History of*
the Colleges and Halls, ed. J. Gutch (1786), p. 248.
A copy of the inscription, cut by Michael Harvey,
was placed over the western entrance to the
Codrington Library in 1978.

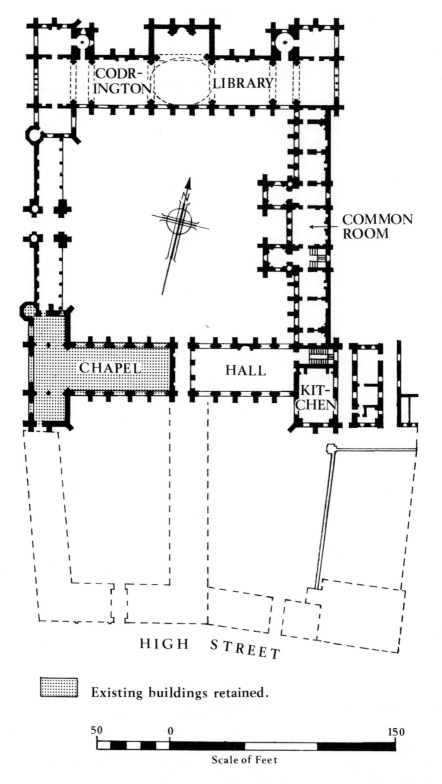

CODR-INGTON LIBRARY

COMMON ROOM

CHAPEL

HALL

KIT-CHEN

HIGH STREET

Existing buildings retained.

50   0   150

Scale of Feet

FIG. 23. Hawksmoor's plan of Feb. 1715. *Redrawn from Worcester College Library, no. 70*

between Hall and Chapel. No drawings survive for these features, which might have been notable examples of Hawksmoor's invention, while the Gothic interior would have been a unique example of its kind at that date. However, Dr Clarke was firmly opposed both to the lanterns and to the idea of a Gothic interior for the Library, and Hawksmoor was obliged to design those ingeniously ambivalent windows — Palladian within and Perpendicular Gothic without — to reconcile the classical interior with the Gothic exterior.

Had the Gothic interior been accepted it is possible that Hawksmoor would have provided some tracery for the side windows, whose large blank areas are one of the least happy features of the building as it exists (Fig. 26). Indeed tracery — though not the Gothic lantern — is shown in one of Hawksmoor's drawings (Fig. 25).

Even the classical interior deviates considerably from what Hawksmoor had in mind. Against the walls he designed two tiers of galleries for the books, and above, a deeply coffered ceiling to subdivide the long single space (Fig. 27). By the time these features came to be executed in the 1740s Hawksmoor was dead, and advice was taken from the architect James Gibbs as to the galleries. He considered that the upper gallery would produce too heavy an effect, and suggested in its place the present arrangement of tall cases with Ionic pilasters surmounted by a row of urns and busts.[16] Although this may well have been an improvement, the ceiling, as executed by the Oxford plasterer Thomas Roberts in 1750–1, was too slight in its projection, and too attenuated in its pattern, to provide an adequate substitute for what Hawksmoor had intended (Fig. 42).

At the same time Townesend was building the new Common Room and the south tower, for which sufficient money had been given by various donors, notably the Earl of Carnarvon (later Duke of Chandos) and Henry Godolphin, Dean of St Paul's and Provost of Eton. Then in 1720 the north tower was begun at the expense of General William Stewart, and soon afterwards the northern and southern flanking blocks were built with money provided by the Duke of Wharton and Sir Nathaniel Lloyd, respectively.[17]

Several drawings illustrate the evolution of the twin towers from lower octagons into the more slender pinnacled turrets which form such an attractive feature of the Oxford skyline (Fig. 28). The idea of flanking the Common Room by two towers grouped together like the west towers of some great medieval church (Beverley was the one that Hawksmoor probably had at the back of his mind, as he had recently been engaged in repairing it), was his

---

[16] Martin, *Catalogue*, p. 296, no. 79a.   [17] All Souls College, Warden's MS 3, fo. 80.

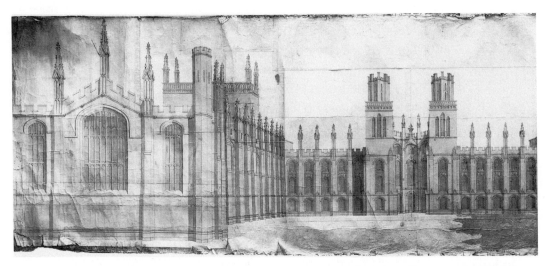

FIG. 24. Perspective of the Codrington Library and North Quadrangle, as proposed by Nicholas Hawksmoor in Feb. 1715. *Bodleian Library, MS Gough Plans 7*

FIG. 25. Design by Nicholas Hawksmoor for the North Quadrangle, showing Gothic tracery in the windows of the Codrington Library. The colonnade of 1703 is shown on the left.
Worcester College Library

FIG. 26. The centre of the Codrington Library, as seen
from the passage between Hall and Chapel

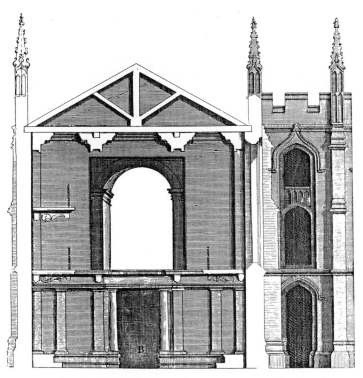

FIG. 27. Section of the Codrington Library as proposed by Hawksmoor,
from an engraving dated 1717

FIG. 28. Hawksmoor's Gothic towers from Malton's *Views of Oxford*
(1802)

solution to the problem of providing a dominant Gothic feature to close the east–west axis. Inevitably twin towers suggest a central entrance, and their only fault is the lack of one. In this respect an earlier version with a concave wall (Fig. 29) might have been preferable. As it is we have the unique conjunction of cathedral towers in a college quadrangle.

The Hall was rebuilt on the new alignment in 1730–3. An engraved plan made in 1721 — no doubt with a view to attracting subscriptions — shows the entrance at the west end, but the College ultimately preferred to have it at the east end, where it could be in the traditional relationship to kitchen and buttery. Surviving correspondence shows how drawings were sent back and forth between Clarke and the 'two men skilled in building', as he called

FIG. 29. Design for the Gothic towers by Hawksmoor made in 1715.
Bodleian Library, MS Gough Plans 7

Hawksmoor and Townesend.[18] Although many drawings were made by Townesend it was Hawksmoor's revisions of them that were generally adopted. The exterior of the Hall had of course to correspond to the Chapel, but for the interior and especially the way the ceiling is handled at each end (Figs. 30, 31), Hawksmoor was largely responsible, and the beautiful coffered

[18] Martin, *Catalogue*, pp. 293–5, nos. 29–51.

(37)

Fig. 30. The interior of the Hall, looking east

ceiling of the buttery (Fig. 33) must be his design, though unfortunately no drawings survive for it. The generosity of those who had contributed to the cost of the Hall was commemorated by shields of their arms painted in the tympanum of the screen and carved on a cartouche outside.[19]

The Ionic columns of the screen were taken from the short-lived cloister of 1703, which had been demolished to make way for a new one designed by Hawksmoor.[20] The northern end of this was built in 1728 with money bequeathed by Sir Peter Mews, but the central gateway and cupola (Fig. 32)

[19] It had originally been intended to include these shields in the decoration of the ceiling (ibid., p. 295, nos. 66b, c).

[20] Ibid., p. 294, no. 42; p. 295, no. 52.

FIG. 31. The interior of the Hall, looking west

and the southern half of the cloister were not built until 1734, with the aid of £750 given by the Hon. Dodington Greville.[21] The two portions differ in detail, and the southern half incorporates what are evidently some more of the columns from the old cloister, economically sawn in half to serve as pilasters, and with new capitals of the Doric Order (Fig. 34). Externally the cloisters and gateway are of course Gothic — in what Hawksmoor called 'the Monastick manner'. But some time after everything else was to be Gothic, he had produced several alternative designs for a gateway 'after the Roman order', just — as he told Dr Clarke — to show that we are 'not quite out of

21 Ibid., p. 295, no. 71.

FIG. 32. The Cloisters, as seen from the North Quadrangle

FIG. 33. The Buttery, showing the coffered ceiling and Hawksmoor's bust

Fig. 34. The interior of the Cloisters, looking south. The rubble masonry on the right probably formed part of the medieval cloister pulled down in 1703

charity with that manner of Building'.[22] One may suspect that he was thinking once more of the Radcliffe Square (or 'Forum Universitatis' as it is called on one of his plans) and of the great new Library which was to be its focal point. Viewed from the College, should the gateway not perhaps be classical to harmonize with Dr Radcliffe's Library? But viewed from the square it obviously ought to harmonize with the College, and was accordingly built in the Gothic style.[23]

[22] 'Explanation'.
[23] When the Radcliffe Square was completed, not everyone was satisfied with the result, and in 1751 the College obtained an estimate for pulling down the cloisters and gateway, presumably with the intention of substituting a simple iron railing (see Martin *Catalogue*, p. 296, no. 99).

FIG. 35. Perspective published in the *Oxford Almanack* for 1728. *Ashmolean Museum, Oxford*

Meanwhile no progress was made with the rebuilding of the Old Quadrangle. Some members of the College evidently still hoped to accomplish this last phase of the grand design, for various versions of it appeared in the Oxford Almanack for 1728 (Fig. 35) and in Williams's *Oxonia depicta* of 1732–3. In these the Library has of course been removed from the Old Quadrangle where Dr Clarke first envisaged it to the North Quadrangle, but the arcade on which it was to have stood remains in Gothic dress and provides a covered way across the quadrangle to a cloister running along the south side of Hall and Chapel and giving access to them both (Fig. 36). But enthusiasm was waning, and at least one potential benefactor was disillusioned by the continuing feuds between the College and its Visitor, on which it had recently wasted no less than £700.[24] This potential benefactor was none other than Dr Clarke, whose will originally left a substantial sum of money 'towards raising and altering

[24] Burrows, *Worthies*, p. 384.

(42)

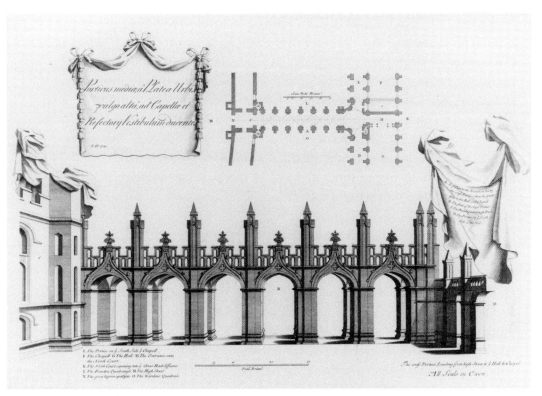

FIG. 36. Design for the Gothic arcade across the Front Quadrangle, from an engraving dated 1721

the Front of All Souls College to the High Street, (according to the printed Design of an Entrance in the middle of it, or according to the Design in Mr. Williams's book of *Oxonia depicta*).'[25]

But in disgust at the College's behaviour he revoked this clause and left the money to build Worcester College instead. When he and Hawksmoor died in 1736, Sir Nathaniel Lloyd, who had once thought of paying for the Gothic arcade across an enlarged Old Quadrangle, told the College that he reckoned 'Hawksmoring and Townsending is all over for this century'.[26]

He was quite right. Nothing more of any architectural consequence was to be done at All Souls for nearly a hundred years. But Codrington's money, Dr Clarke's guidance, and Hawksmoor's genius had combined to give Oxford one of its great Gothic monuments — a building as notable in its time as the Divinity School had been in the fifteenth century or as the University Museum was to be in the nineteenth.

But how are we to place Hawksmoor's work at All Souls in English

---

[25] *A True Copy of the Last Will and Testament of George Clarke, Esq., LL D* (1737).

[26] Letter to the Warden dated 8 Nov. 1736 (Martin, *Catalogue*, p. 299, no. 39).

architectural history? Architectural historians have never found it easy to put Hawksmoor's Gothic into any recognized category. At Oxford we have much Persistent or Traditional Gothic, notably at Wadham, Mannerist Gothic at Brasenose, Rational or Royal Society Gothic at Christ Church (Tom Tower), Antiquarian Gothic (now destroyed) at University College, Dogmatic Gothic at Exeter, Muscular Gothic at Keble, Scholarly Gothic at Pusey House. Hawksmoor's Gothic fits none of these categories. Traditional it certainly is not. It is anything but rational and not in the least antiquarian. Neither is it scholarly, still less dogmatic. How are we to evaluate it? In what spirit was it designed?

I have tried to show that the use of the Gothic style at All Souls is to be explained chiefly by the principle of conformity that had led Wren to design a Gothic Tom Tower at Christ Church, where he 'resolved it ought to be Gothick to agree with the Founder's worke.'[27] So paradoxically it was the Renaissance idea of consistency in style — of avoiding what Wren called 'an unhandsome medley', that pointed to a Gothic rather than a classical design. But whereas Wren regretted that at Christ Church he was prevented from adopting what he called 'a better form of Architcture', I think we can conclude that Hawksmoor saw in Gothic an opportunity to achieve with a different vocabulary those dramatic and scenic effects that appealed to him as a baroque architect. It has often been remarked how in his London churches Hawksmoor created with classical components — columns, pilasters, even Roman altars — effects similar to those of Gothic steeples, and here at All Souls he found himself using the Gothic vocabulary itself.

It was a vocabulary of which he was, of course, ignorant in a scholarly sense: indeed, when it came to details, he scarcely knew the difference between Romanesque and Gothic, let alone between different periods of Gothic, so that at All Souls we find elements of quite different phases of medieval architecture mixed up together in a way which was to distress and infuriate the more pedantic minds of nineteenth-century critics, nurtured in the Gothic Revival.[28]

But Hawksmoor could see the possibilities of tower and pinnacle as well as any Gothic Revivalist, and his total lack of archaeological inhibition enabled him to exploit them with a bravado of which few Gothic Revivalists would have been capable. Like some post-Modernist of the 1980s rediscovering

---

[27] W. D. Caröe, *Wren and Tom Tower* (1923), p. 23.

[28] In 1872 C. L. Eastlake castigated Hawksmoor's work at All Souls as 'the most debased travesty of Pointed architecture in Oxford' (*The Gothic Revival*, p. 102). For A. Vallance in 1912 it was 'a puerile caricature of the kind that only brings the noble name of Gothic into contempt' (*The Old Colleges of Oxford*, p. 48).

Fɪɢ. 37. Bust of Nicholas Hawksmoor at
All Souls College by Sir Henry Cheere
John Haywood

Fɪɢ. 38. Monument to Dr George Clarke in the
Chapel

classical architecture after a lifetime in the concrete wilderness, Hawksmoor seized on the salient features of a half-forgotten style and exploited them without any pretensions to scholarship.

The result is something unique: Gothic used scenically and romantically, but within the conventions of a classical tradition which insisted on symmetry and would not permit the kind of deliberately irregular grouping which was to be exploited by James Wyatt sixty or seventy years later. Vanbrugh of course saw similar possibilities in the towers and bastions of military architecture, but he never used overtly Gothic features to give what he called a 'castle air' to his houses.

Indeed the only parallel to Hawksmoor's baroque Gothic (for that is what I think we must call it) is to be found in Bohemia in the work of his contemporary the Czech architect Jan Santini Aichel (1677–1723).[29] Santini was an architect trained in the German baroque tradition who exploited his native Gothic architecture for baroque ends. In Bohemia the fantasies of late Gothic architecture lent themselves easily to baroque interpretation. In England Hawksmoor had a much more rectilinear tradition to start from: carefully compartmented rather than interpenetrating spaces, Perpendicular rather than flamboyant tracery. But that was no problem, for his classical architecture tends also to be built up out of cubical rather than plastic elements.

So in the North Quadrangle at All Souls we have a unique episode in English architecture — English collegiate Gothic seen through baroque eyes: an episode which we, in the late twentieth century, freed at last from the antiquarian inhibitions of the Gothic Revival, are probably better able to appreciate than any generation since the one that first saw it built.

[29] For Santini Aichel see N. Pevsner, 'Bohemian Hawksmoor', *Architectural Review* cxxi (Feb. 1957), A. K. Placzek (ed.), *Macmillan Encyclopaedia of Architecture*, iii (1982), pp. 660–3, and B. Queysanne *et al.*, *J. B. Santini-Aichl, Un Architecte baroque–gothique en Bohême* (École d'architecture de Grenoble, 1986), with further bibliography. His principal Gothic works are the abbey church of Sedlec (1703–6), the neighbouring cemetery chapel (1708–12), the west front of the abbey church at Kladruby (1712–16), and the pilgrimage church of St John Nepomuc at Žďár (1719–22).

3

From Hawksmoor to Sir George Gilbert Scott

THE year 1750 is both a convenient and a significant date in the architectural history of All Souls. It marks the bitter end of the 'Hawksmoring and Town-sending' that had kept the College in a state of architectural upheaval for almost half a century. In that year its great new Library became at last a working library rather than a mere library room, and the Wardens and fellows could face a future rich in academic promise. But though they may have been men of taste and breeding, few of them (with the notable exception of William Blackstone, fellow from 1743–62) had scholarly pretensions. For example, from 1750 until Sir William Anson's election as the College's first lay Warden in 1881, no Warden of All Souls is known to have added to the general stock of human knowledge by publishing a book. And though the roll of Wardens starts with the unusually plebeian Stephen Niblett (elected in 1727), the names of his successors leave one in no doubt about their social standing.[1] They run: Viscount Tracy (1766), Edward Isham (1793), the Hon. Edward Legge (1817), Lewis Sneyd (1827), and Francis Knyvett Leighton (1858). Whether married or single, they occupied the Lodgings, and each election can be said to have had an architectural impact since it involved the College in expenditure on alterations to the Lodgings. In the case of Warden Leighton in 1858 the College spent £1,800 on alterations and on a substantial wing in the Gothic style.[2]

Chichele's statutory figure of forty fellows stood until the Commissioners' Ordinance of 1857 when their numbers were temporarily reduced by ten in order to provide funds to finance the College's Chichele Professors. These held the chairs of International Law and Diplomacy and of Modern History, established in 1859 and 1862 respectively. It is perhaps unsurprising that their holders had to wait until 1870 before they were admitted to fellowships.

The social and intellectual tone of the College during the period did much

---

[1] Niblett was not even armigerous, and the patent of arms granted to him on 3 June 1732 (six years after his election as Warden) is in the College Archives (C. T. Martin, *Catalogue of the Archives in the Muniment Rooms of All Souls College* (1877), p. 400, no. 325). Hereafter documents in the College archives are cited by reference to the inter-leaved copy of Martin in the Codrington Library at All Souls.

[2] All Souls College, *Acta in Capitulis*, 1851–92 (MS 401(e)), 25 Mar. 1858, 15 June 1859.

to justify the *bene nati, bene vestiti, mediocriter docti* gibe which outsiders were happy to launch against its fellows.[3] Between 1750 and 1857 more than half of those elected belonged to the charmed circle of families who could take advantage of the 'founder's kin' privilege in elections. It is significant that forty per cent of the fellows came from Christ Church and only eight per cent from Balliol — and only three of the latter before Jowett's 'colonizing' influence became dominant in the 1840s. Such men were in easy circumstances and often contrived to be non-resident for long periods. When Macaulay visited All Souls in October 1854 he found Warden Leighton to be the only 'Soul' in residence.[4] Even their attendance at College Meetings could be irregular, and as late as 1880 W. P. Ker's and J. R. Maguire's fellowship admission ceremony had to be repeated when it was discovered that only two fellows had been present on the original occasion. But we will see that this kind of detachment did not mean that the fellows did not hold strong opinions when religious and aesthetic questions arose.

On the *mediocriter docti* side the cap fitted — though not perfectly, and not after the 'revolution' of 1857, when the Commissioners' Ordinance swept away the founder's kin privilege and demanded a first class in the Schools or a University prize as a precondition of candidacy for the fellowship examination. From 1800, when the honours system was established, until 1856 only eighteen of the 149 fellows elected had first classes. Seven of these were founder's kin — a proportion of only seven per cent as against the twenty-one per cent of first classes among those elected who did not enjoy the privilege.[5]

In view of what I have said on the *bene nati* theme I regard myself as absolved from commenting on the *bene vestiti* one: it is something that we may take for granted. There is, however, one area of critical importance — and of architectural significance — which the old gibe omits: the religious side of the College's life. Perhaps this, too, was taken for granted, for Chichele intended his College to be a nursery for a learned clergy — a *militia* to serve church and state — and the obligation to take Holy Orders was originally strict. Later on ingenuity was exercised to circumvent the statute — particularly from the eighteenth century onwards — but even so the figures (certainly imperfect) show that more than half the fellows during the period 1750–1880 were clerics. There were two chaplains throughout the period,

---

[3] The slur seems to be first recorded in Thomas Fuller, *Church-History of Britain* (1655), book 4, p. 182. The basis for it must be the qualifications for fellowship required by the original College statutes (chap. 1): '... rudimentis grammaticae sufficienter ... eruditi ... de legitimo matrimonio nati, bonis conditionibus et moribus perornati ...'.

[4] T. B. Macaulay, *Letters*, ed. T. Pinney, v (1981), p. 423.

[5] Compare Oriel College over the same period: over two-thirds of the elections to fellowships there were of 'first-class men' (G. C. Richards and C. L. Shadwell, *The Provosts and Fellows of Oriel College, Oxford* (1922)).

choristers appear in the records until 1815, and the three clerks (later four Bible Clerks) assisted in the daily Chapel services, and in earlier days performed menial duties such as waiting at table.[6] The tone of the College was overtly religious — high and dry, and matching its social tone. It seems to have been little affected by the Oxford Movement though two fellows, Gilbert Talbot and John Henry Wynne, went over to Rome in 1851 at the time of the Gorham case; and Edward Dean, the future brother-in-law of the Blessed Fanny Taylor, followed them in 1855. Even so, against such a background questions relating to the Chapel were unlikely to prove to be neutral issues.

Such were the *dramatis personae*: I must now turn to what they did in the architectural line during the century and a quarter after 1750.

The year 1750, as I have remarked, was the year of the completion of the shelving of the Codrington Library. Books could at last be removed from storage rooms and from the groaning shelves in the Old Library to the yawning cavern of Hawksmoor's magnificent construction. In 1751 the Old Library was allotted to a law fellow, Robert Vansittart.[7] The room was partitioned and two fireplaces were constructed in it, but the face-ends of the Elizabethan presses were mercifully retained; they were placed between the window splays, and a considerable amount of Strawberry Hill Gothick panelling was used to line the walls of the rooms.[8]

Two years later the Gothick passion still raged, and in August 1753 orders were given for a Gothick pavilion to be erected in the College garden (presumably what is now the Fellows' Garden). Sadly, by 1789 it had so decayed (and the Gothick impulse had so declined) that orders were given for it to be removed. Fortunately the plaster high-relief of the College's mallard totem which had graced it, was preserved and now has the College buttery under its wing.[9] In the 1760s money was well spent on repairs to the front quadrangle — which was, incidentally, paved, and all the better for being so.[10]

---

[6] The last election to Bible clerkships was in 1921. Cf. R. E. Eason and R. A. Snoxall, *The Last of their Line: The Bible Clerks of All Souls College, Oxford* (1976).

[7] MS 401(b), 10 Aug. 1750. The entry is reproduced in facsimile in J. S. G. Simmons, *Doctor Johnson and All Souls* (1975), p. 5.

[8] For the presses see B. H. Streeter, *The Chained Library* (1931), p. 171, corrected by H. H. E. Craster, *The History of All Souls College Library*, ed. E. F. Jacob (1971), pp. 49–52. It was presumably in these converted rooms that Vansittart entertained Dr Johnson to tea in July 1759 (see Boswell's *Life of Johnson*, ed. Hill-Powell, i (1934), p. 347). Dr

Colvin reminds me that Sanderson Miller planned the conversion for Vansittart (see Vansittart's letters to Miller in the Warwickshire Record Office: CR 125B/715–20, 10 Sept. 1750–21 Aug. 1751).

[9] MS 401(c), 22 Aug. 1753, 4 June 1789.

[10] MS 401(c), 3 Apr. 1760, 26 Nov. 1762, 29 Aug. 1765. The last entry also records the laying of an 'oval grass-plat' in the North Quadrangle. Note that Isaac Taylor's Oxford map of 1751 and Richard Davis's of 1797 both show the Quadrangle traversed by broad east–west and north–south paths crossing at its centre.

FIG. 39. The east end of the Chapel, 1716–73, from the painting by 'Green' referred to in the
will of Dr George Clarke. *All Souls College*

Fig. 40. The east end of Magdalen College Chapel showing Isaac Fuller's 'Resurrection', *c.* 1665, with (below) the 'Christ carrying the Cross' installed in 1745, and the panelling and surround of 1758. *Lithograph by G. Cooper, 1817*

The end of the 1760s was marked by a distinctly un-Gothick enterprise affecting the east end of the Chapel. George Clarke's gift in 1714 of panelling and of a pedimented wooden altar-piece for the east end of the Chapel included an ornamental marble central feature (Fig. 39) which some evidently thought cried out for improvement. Magdalen had pioneered in Oxford the rather un-English idea of incorporating a devotional picture into the east end of its Chapel, placing there in 1745 a large 'Christ bearing the Cross' (attributed by T. S. R. Boase to Valdés Leal) which, significantly enough, was booty from Vigo in Spain in 1702 (Fig. 40).[11] Other colleges, Corpus, Merton, Queen's, Pembroke, and University took up the fashion and All Souls also followed the trend. In 1769 an order was placed for a large *Noli me tangere* (Fig. 41) from the highly fashionable painter, Raphael Mengs, then working in Madrid. Mengs later moved to Rome and had completed the picture there by September 1771. Its cost with extras amounted to £422 and the College expended over a thousand pounds more in refurbishing the Chapel — which became one of the sights of Oxford.[12] The picture and its setting continued to excite the sensibilities of visitors for several decades — in fact until the Gothic Revival of the 1830s.

The new century was to see two major architectural efforts — in the 1820s and in the 1870s — but it began with a whimper. In 1804 it was decided to simplify Thomas Roberts's plaster ceiling and attic decorations in the Codrington (Fig. 42) by removing almost all of them (one guesses that the decision was a reaction to a fall of plaster rather than a piece of flotsam swept in on the tide of taste);[13] and in 1817, the year in which the Bishop of Oxford, Edward Legge (who had been a fellow from 1789–1805), was elected Warden, an extension was added at the west end of the Lodgings. This was, incidentally, to be succeeded by the more ambitious wing already referred to, which was added in 1858 when Warden Leighton took up office.

The first architectural *démarche* of the 1820s was one of those developments that ministered to the social needs of the fellows — an undistinguished coffee-room built in 1824 under the direction of Samuel Benham, an architect then working in Oxford.[14] This is the existing room to the south east of the eastern

---

[11] The picture is discussed and illustrated in T. S. R. Boase, *Christ Bearing the Cross, attributed to Valdés Leal* (Charlton Lectures on Art, 1954).

[12] J. H. A. Sparrow, 'An Oxford Altar-Piece', *Burlington Magazine*, cii (1960), 4–9, 452–5; cvii (1965), 631–2.

[13] All Souls College, Library Committee Minute Book, 12 May 1804. Fig. 42 reproduces Thomas Malton's aquatint of 1802 which shows the plaster

decoration applied to the ceiling compartments and to the north wall above the cornice in 1750. All this work was removed except for the Chichele heraldic achievement which remains on the attic wall of the recess behind the statue of Codrington.

[14] MS 401(d), 17 Dec. 1823. For Benham see Colvin, *Biographical Dictionary of British Architects, 1600–1840* (1978), p. 107.

FIG. 41. *Noli me tangere*, painted by
Raphael Mengs, 1769–71, and installed at
the east end of the Chapel in 1773. *All
Souls College, on loan to the Ashmolean
Museum, Oxford*

FIG. 42. The interior of the Codrington
Library from the south east, showing
Roberts's plaster ceiling and attic
decorations of 1750, removed in 1804.
Aquatint by T. Malton, 1802

range of the North Quadrangle. Individual fellows gave a mantelpiece and furniture for the room, and four portraits were presented to the Hall. The College evidently had the bit between its teeth: by the end of 1825 it was contemplating major works, the restoration and improvement of the High Street and the Catte Street fronts (the latter as far as the Chapel).

In March 1826 the fellows were examining plans and accepted one of several submitted by the architect Daniel Robertson at a £2,500 plus fees estimate.[15] In February 1827 they also accepted one of Robertson's plans for restoring the Warden's Lodgings at £695.[16] Why Daniel Robertson was chosen by the College is uncertain — he is said to have drawn best when excited with sherry — but he was the man on the spot, being at the time in charge of the new Walton Street building of the Clarendon Press — an assignment from which he was later withdrawn after an unspecified local scandal.[17] Be that as it may, he produced a number of drawings of the All Souls street front and the Lodgings. Most of these are in the Soane Museum together with a large file of papers concerning the job.[18] They are there because of another scandal — this time of a specific kind — in which Sir John Soane was asked to arbitrate. What happened is that the local contractor entrusted with the work at All Souls, James Johnson, appealed to the College, having found himself quite unable to keep within the £2,500 estimate that Daniel Robertson had prepared for refacing in Bath stone — a figure which Johnson had accepted without question.[19] Sir John Soane found that Daniel Robertson had in any case made an error of £1,000 in his arithmetic and that the true estimate should have been nearer £5,000 than £2,500. From the graphic evidence preserved in connection with the scandal we can see that Robertson's ideas for the street front as far as the Lodgings involved the regular gothicization of the existing elevation (Figs. 43–4). The sash windows introduced by Warden Finch in 1687 gave way to oriels and various Gothic elaborations. Chimneys and dormers were made uniform, and the former are handsomely decorated with blind tracery in the Tudor manner. For the more domestic Lodgings he offered elevations in Houses-of-Parliament Gothic or in the Palladian manner (Figs. 45–6). The College plumped for the latter with a rusticated lower storey and a classical balustrade and window architraves.[20]

As a result of Robertson's efforts the College frontages took on the

---

[15] MS 401(d), 30 Mar. 1826.
[16] Ibid., 19 Feb. 1827.
[17] Colvin, *Biographical Dictionary*, p. 697.
[18] Sir John Soane's Museum, Div. VIII. M (papers); ibid., 73.1 (drawings).
[19] MS 401(d), 24 Dec. 1827.

[20] It is these alterations of the 1820s that must have misled the authors of the Oxfordshire volume in the *Buildings of England* series into characterizing George Clarke's Lodgings as 'the first piece of Palladianism in Oxfordshire and probably in England' (p. 98).

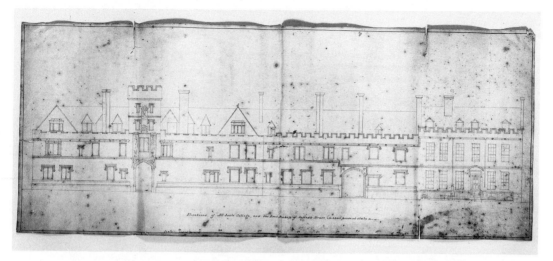

FIG. 43. High Street front: elevation before restoration. *Drawing by Daniel Robertson, 1826. All Souls College Archives*

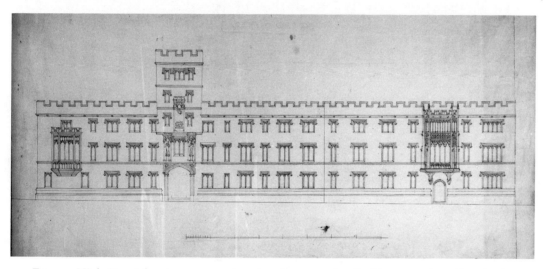

FIG. 44. High Street front: unexecuted project for a regular Gothic restoration. *Drawing by Daniel Robertson, 1826. Sir John Soane's Museum*

character that they have today, but when the interior and exterior decorative activities of the 1820s terminated with the settlement of the Robertson–Johnson affair in 1829 (the College having agreed to pay the difference), the Fellows must have sighed with relief.[21]

Conservation work continued, however. In 1836 and 1837 the twin towers were repaired and cased in Bath stone and new windows were put into both

---

[21] MS 401(d), 17 Dec. 1828.

FIG. 45. Warden's Lodgings: unexecuted Gothic project for the High Street front. *Drawing by Daniel Robertson, 1827. All Souls College Archives*

towers and into the passage in the range to the south of them.[22] The former year also saw Mr Wyatt, a local builder and plumber much patronized by the College, receiving over £600 for converting the 'present Necessaries into water closets' (for plumbed baths the fellows had to wait until the twentieth century).[23]

In 1838 concern was shown for a less down-to-earth matter — the Codrington Library. What is now the Sub-Librarian's room was fitted up with shelving and with a spiral staircase giving access to three galleried floors — the work being done (again by Wyatt) to an estimate of £300.[24]

Twenty years later the academic reforms of the early 1850s and the

[22] Ibid., 3 Sept. 1836, 26 Dec. 1837.
[23] Ibid., 16 Apr. 1836.
[24] Library Committee Minute Book, 18 Apr. 1838. The west gallery was removed in 1876 in order to 'enhance the light' in the room (ibid., 7 June 1876); it has recently had to be reinstated — to enhance the safety of readers and staff.

FIG. 46. Warden's Lodgings: the Palladian High Street front as executed. A plain entablature later replaced the balustraded one. *Drawing by Daniel Robertson, 1827. Sir John Soane's Museum*

Ordinance of 1857 made their influence felt in a greater awareness of the College's academic responsibilities, and in 1858 an unsuccessful attempt was made to open the Library to out-College readers.[25] However, early in 1867 one of the fellows, C. H. Robarts — a fiery particle who at one time favoured the amalgamation of All Souls with the Bodleian and who had the distinction of once having proposed to a College Meeting thirty notices of motion (some of them sensible, but none of which was considered) — had a surprising success: he persuaded the College to open its Library to the University at large, and to build a reading-room for out-College readers on All Souls land at the back of the Great Library and east of the room in which the spiral staircase had been installed thirty years before.[26] This is what we now know as the Anson Reading-Room and its construction was a landmark: it confirmed the College specialization in law and its then academically connected discipline, modern history. It is a cosy Victorian room, built by Wyatt to the design of E. G. Bruton, a prolific local architect. The insertion in 1885 of a gallery (also designed by Bruton) has not spoiled it.

Robarts's sensible idea of an entrance to the Library from Radcliffe Square

[25] MS 401(f), 17 Dec. 1858.
[26] All Souls College Minute Book, 1858–75 (MS 401(f), 26 Feb. 1867).

suffered the fate of most of his suggestions and the existing entrance was not contrived until eight years later, in 1876.[27]

By 1876 the College was deeply involved in its second major architectural campaign — the Chapel restoration.

That something needed to be done is clear from a manuscript in the Bodleian in which Miss Charlotte Elizabeth White of Kensington, visiting Oxford in the autumn of 1845, wrote of the Chapel: 'Everything seemed to me in bad taste. Everything, columns, walls, pilasters, stalls, all painted a dark, dingy, melancholy olive green — which, in Oxford, goes by the name of the "All Souls colour".'[28]

Now what had Miss White seen that had engendered this state of revulsion? The upper part of the east wall of the Chapel was graced by Thornhill's 'Apotheosis of Archbishop Chichele' of 1715–16, overlaying Isaac Fuller's fresco Resurrection of the 1660s.[29] Below it was Dr Clarke's classical panelling of 1714, with its pedimented central altar-piece framing the Mengs *Noli me tangere*, finally installed in 1773 (Fig. 47). Between the ten side windows of the chancel were giant *trompe l'œil* figures of the four Latin Fathers (the dedicatees of the Chapel) and of archbishops and Lancastrian notables; two large *trompe l'œil* vases (representing the sacraments) completed Thornhill's decorative scheme of 1715–16.[30] At the west end of the chancel was the screen (Fig. 48) that Thornhill had redesigned in 1716 on the basis of the 1660s' one — the latter traditionally attributed to Christopher Wren.[31] Had Miss White lifted up her eyes to the roof of the chancel she would have seen in the spaces between the trusses Thornhill's *trompe l'œil* coffering painted on canvas in 1716 and concealing the figures painted on board by Isaac Fuller which had been installed as part of the Restoration Chapel improvements.[32] A successful effort had in fact been made in the early eighteenth century to classicize the Chapel, and Miss White's distaste may well have been in part due to the fact that she visited All Souls after visiting New College and Magdalen (Figs. 49–

---

[27] Library Committee Report, Dec. 1876.

[28] Bodleian Library, MS Eng. misc. e. 1517, fo. 26 (entry for 10 Sept. 1845). My thanks are due to Bodley's Librarian for drawing my attention to this recently acquired manuscript.

[29] John Evelyn saw (and disapproved of) Fuller's recently completed fresco on 25 Oct. 1664 (*Diary*, ed. E. S. de Beer, iii (1955), pp. 385–6).

[30] It is worth remarking that the decorative scheme (less the irrelevant archbishops and Lancastrian notables) was repeated by Thornhill ten years later in the Chapel at Wimpole near Cambridge. There was an appropriateness about this,

as the Wimpole estate had been in the hands of the Chichele family from the fifteenth century until 1686.

[31] See the project for a screen incorporating Archbishop Chichele's coat of arms (Wren Society, v (1928), pl. 7); also Colvin, *A Catalogue of Architectural Drawings of the Eighteenth and Nineteenth Centuries in the Library of Worcester College, Oxford* (1964), no. 47, pl. 82.

[32] K. Downes, 'Fuller's Last Judgement', *Burlington Magazine*, cii (1960), 450–2; M. R. Toynbee, 'Robert Streater and All Souls College Chapel', *Oxoniensia*, viii–ix (1943–4), 205.

Fig. 47. The east end of the Chapel showing Dr George Clarke's panelling and pedimented central feature (1714) framing the *Noli me tangere* (1769–71), with Thornhill's fresco 'Apotheosis of Archbishop Chichele' (1715–16) above and his *trompe l'œil* wall-figures, vases, and ceiling-coffering of the same years. *Lithograph by G. Cooper, 1817. Bodleian Library*

50) — both of which colleges had neo-Gothic reredoses — and classicism was in any case no longer the thing in Oxford in the 1840s.

A quarter of a century or so after Miss White's 1845 visit the state of the Chapel had not improved, and in May 1869 it was decided to invite an architect to survey it and to prepare plans and estimates for its restoration. The chosen architect was Henry Clutton — a man we know a good deal about thanks to Dr Pamela Hunting's researches.[33]

[33] 'The Life and Work of Henry Clutton, 1819–1893' (Ph.D. thesis, Bedford College, University of London, 1979). A microfilm of this study, to which I am much indebted, is in the Bodleian (Diss. Films 829).

FIG. 48. The Chapel viewed from the east end showing Thornhill's screen, 1716. *Unfinished aquatint plate by T. Malton, 1802–4, published by M. Malton in 1810. Bodleian Library*

    Why he was chosen it is impossible to say. The College Minutes record that in May 1860 an unsuccessful approach to the College had been made by a 'Mr. Clutton' for assistance in building a church at Hartswood, Surrey.[34] But this was *another* architect of the same name whose life overlapped that of the 'All Souls Clutton' and a man whose existence does nothing to simplify the work of architectural historians. *Our* Henry Clutton had been a pupil (with William Burges) of Edward Blore and with Burges had won an international competition with a Gothic design for Lille Cathedral in 1856. He had done a good deal of Anglican cathedral restoration until his conversion to Roman Catholicism in the same year. Four years later, in 1860, he married one of the

---

[34] MS 401(f), 18 May 1869.

Fig. 49. The east end of New College Chapel showing
Bernato Bernasconi's plaster reredos installed as part of James
Wyatt's remodelling of the Chapel interior in 1789–94.
Rebuilt in stone by Sir Gilbert Scott (1877–81), it remained
without statuary until 1892. *Aquatint by T. Malton, 1803.*
Bodleian Library

future Cardinal Manning's nieces and thereafter did much ecclesiastical and
secular work, principally for the Roman Catholic hierarchy and laymen. He
had built the Oratory School in Birmingham for Newman in 1858, and
Newman had marked him down as the architect for his abortive Oratorian
college in Oxford in 1864.[35] A tenuous All Souls link is that in 1859 he had
built a house near Southampton for Sir Edward Hulse (an Anglican) who had
been an influential fellow of All Souls from 1829–53.

This stress on Clutton's religious proclivities may seem excessive, but it is
not irrelevant: the late 1860s was the period of the Ritual Commission and 1871

[35] J. H. Newman, *Letters and Diaries*, ed. C. S. Dessain and E. E. Kelly, xxi (1971), 540.

Fig. 50. The east end of Magdalen College Chapel showing the reredos inserted by L. N. Cottingham as part of his gothicization of the chapel, 1829–35. The niches were filled with statues of Old Testament figures (plus St John the Baptist) in 1864. *Lithograph by F. Bedford, 1845. Bodleian Library*

saw the admission of dissenters to non-theological degrees at Oxford. The religious atmosphere was tense, and it was a narrow safe path that ran between the ornate Scylla of Ritualism and the bare Charybdis of Low Church and dissent. There was, moreover, in the College a clash between the proponents of the Gothic and the classical (or 'Italian') styles. However, at first all went well. Clutton presented his Chapel report within three weeks (in June 1869).[36]

---

[36] Unless otherwise indicated, the story of the Chapel restoration is based on the Reports of the Chapel Restoration Committee and other materials in the College Minute Books (MSS 401(f) and (g)) and on Clutton's privately printed *Narrative and Correspondence Relating to the Restoration of All Souls College Chapel, May 18, 1872* (copy in the Bodleian: GA Oxon. 8° 957).

He proposed full restoration of the roof and of the exterior walls (particularly on the south). As regards the interior he suggested alternatives: (1) leave it what he termed 'Italian', (2) restore the Gothic and Gothicize the Italian, and (3) fully restore in the Gothic manner including a Gothic screen to replace Thornhill's baroque one. He also reminded the fellows that behind the Thornhill fresco and Dr Clarke's panelling and the Mengs picture there probably lay concealed what he described as 'the skeleton of the Celebrated reredos, which rose from floor to ceiling'.

Nine months after receiving Clutton's report the College Bursar had to confide to him in a letter that 'it is very difficult to move a body like us', and it was not until nearly a year later, in February 1871, that the College asked Clutton to prepare drawings and specifications for restoration work on the fabric, i.e. on the exterior walls and roof of the Chapel. In April 1871 he was at last authorized to proceed, and the work was completed in Bath stone with Ketton pinnacles by December 1871.[37] In that month, the College instructed him to attend to the interior of the Chapel, ordering the removal of Thornhill's *trompe l'œil* ceiling coffering, painted on canvas and masking the figures painted on board by Isaac Fuller; the latter were also removed. In January 1872 he was asked to produce plans for a Gothic screen, and for the restoration of the fifteenth-century stalls, but nothing was said about the reredos, part of which had been revealed by the removal (by Clutton) of some of the ornamental marble at the east end of the Chapel. Clutton proceeded with the work but over-enthusiastically included when reporting to the College in March 'an estimate of the probable cost for restoring such a work as the reredos without filling the niches' — for it was evident that the reredos was bare of statuary and had been cut back when Fuller's fresco had been applied to it in the 1660s (Fig. 51). Then the blow fell: on 13 April 1872 the Secretary of the Chapel Restoration Committee wrote to him telling him that his services were no longer required as there was 'a general feeling against placing such a work as the restoration of the newly-discovered reredos in the hands of any architect whose views are not formed on the same theological basis as that of the members of the College.'

Clutton protested vehemently in a privately printed *Narrative* that his religious faith had not changed since his appointment in 1869 and that it had been known to members of the Chapel Restoration Committee. His protests were in vain.

It is difficult to decide whether the religious issue was the only, or only

---

[37] *The Builder* (21 Oct. 1871), 830; see also ibid. (16 Jan. 1875), 63 and (4 Nov. 1876), 1078 for progress reports.

FIG. 51. The east end of the Chapel as revealed in 1872 after the removal of the Thornhill fresco, the Mengs picture with its pedimented frame, and George Clarke's panelling on either side of the altar and on the north and south walls. *Photograph, 1872. Bodleian Library*

the main, stumbling-block for Clutton. Certainly Montagu Burrows, the Chichele Professor of Modern History and the man who confirmed in the autumn of 1871 the presence of the reredos which Clutton had referred to a couple of years earlier, was an influential member of the Chapel Committee and a staunch anti-Ritualist Church-of-England man.[38] On the other hand, it is difficult to reconcile Clutton's dismissal on religious grounds with the fact that the sculptor who was eventually to fill the bare ruined niches of the reredos with graven images was a naturalized Pole who was surely a Roman

[38] M. Burrows, *The Worthies of All Souls* (1874), p. vi.

Catholic, and that the man who was almost immediately appointed to replace Clutton as Chapel architect, George Gilbert Scott, was the man involved in a controversy which eventually went to the Privy Council in connection with so-called 'superstitious images' put up under his direction in Exeter Cathedral.[39]

To pass from speculation to hard facts. One fact was that the Thornhill fresco and the *Noli me tangere* were now redundant. Their fate was to be very partial preservation in the case of the Thornhill, and banishment to a position distinctly 'above the line' on the south wall of the antechapel for the Mengs picture.[40] An even harder fact was that the 'cut-back' medieval reredos had been revealed without statuary and that very considerable expense would be needed to make it presentable. In the emergency the Senior Fellow, Lord Bathurst, came to the rescue of the College. In May 1872 he offered to pay for the restoration of the reredos and at the same College Meeting it was proposed that George Gilbert Scott be approached to prepare designs and estimates. Bathurst's generous offer was accepted with gratitude and Scott's appointment was confirmed in the following December.[41]

The man whose appointment the College then confirmed was known in Oxford as the architect of the Martyrs' Memorial and of Exeter College Chapel, and he had been working on the restoration of the east end of Oxford Cathedral since 1870. His works elsewhere were legion and included St John's College Chapel, Cambridge, the St Pancras Hotel, and the Albert Memorial. The last of these had recently been opened to the public (in July 1872) and George Gilbert Scott had become Sir Gilbert in the following month. His skill — and determination — as a restorer were legendary, and the establishment of the Society for the Protection of Ancient Buildings is said to have been not unconnected with his activities.[42]

Sir Gilbert Scott had an enormously busy office but he lost no time in taking over after his appointment in December 1872, and by Easter 1873 had furnished plans for restoring the great reredos (Fig. 52), the sedilia and stalls, and providing a Gothic screen (Fig. 53) to replace the baroque one. For the last of these subscriptions were mercifully inadequate, but contracts were

[39] *Phillpotts* v. *Boyd* (1875), LR 6 PC 435.

[40] Some fragments of the Thornhill fresco survive and are located on the staircase at the west end of the Codrington Library. The Fuller fresco that underlay the Thornhill has disappeared, but some fragments of his ceiling paintings on board are over the door into the antechapel. The Mengs picture is at present (1988) on loan to the Ashmolean Museum.

[41] Lord Bathurst's total personal contribution amounted to about £2,000. A grateful College

perpetuated him as the northernmost figure in the bottom range of reredos statues; Lord Salisbury, quondam fellow and Chancellor of the University, appears (as 'John of Gaunt') on the south side of the altar (the third figure in the same row, reading from the south).

[42] *Dictionary of National Biography*, li (1897), p. 22; D. Cole includes in his *Work of Sir Gilbert Scott* (1980) a list of about a thousand buildings with which Scott was associated.

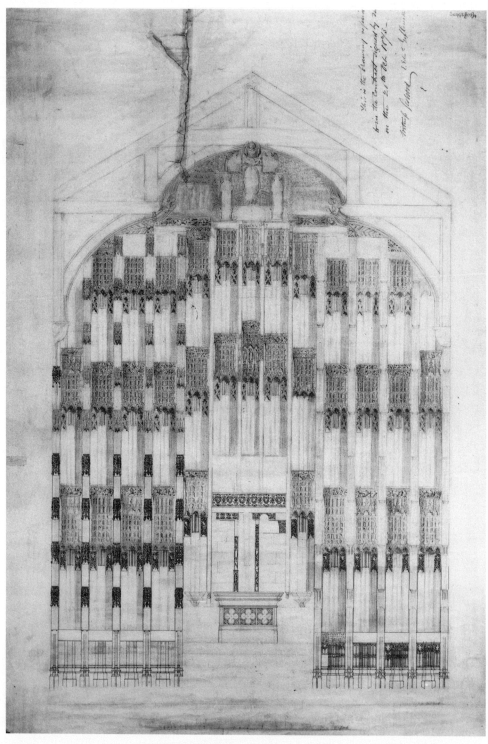

FIG. 52. The Chapel: Sir Gilbert Scott's drawing of the reredos signed by the sculptor E. E. Geflowski on 20 Oct. 1873, and showing the surviving old work and the new canopies, tabernacle-work, etc. *British Architectural Library*

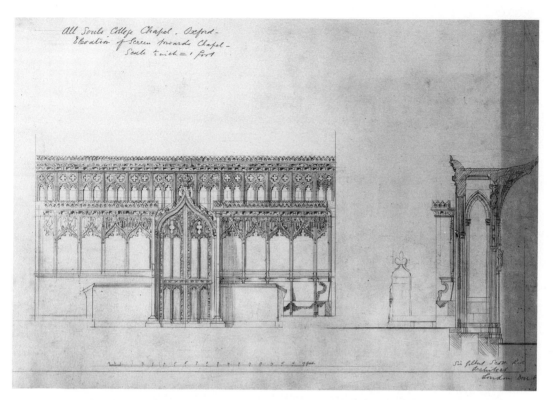

FIG. 53. The Chapel: the east elevation of Sir Gilbert Scott's unexecuted project for a Gothic screen to replace Thornhill's 1716 screen at the west end of the chancel. Dated 8 Dec. 1875. *All Souls College Archives*

signed for all the rest of the work during the summer of 1873.

Scott now turned his attention to the figures for the reredos, and it was probably either at his or Bathurst's suggestion that the Polish *émigré* sculptor, Emanuel Edward Gawłowski (Geflowski as he was known in England) was entrusted with the work. We know a good deal about Geflowski thanks to the researches of Mieczysław Paszkiewicz and of Wiesław Toporowski, of Oxford.[43] He had become a naturalized British subject in 1867. He exhibited at the Academy in that and in subsequent years, and he made a plaster bust of Mountague Bernard, the Chichele Professor of International Law and a fellow of All Souls, in 1873.[44] In October 1873 Geflowski signed a contract

[43] M. Paszkiewicz, 'Rzezby Edwarda Gawłow-skiego w Anglii', *Muzeum Polskie*, 5 (London, 1975), 193–200; W. Toporowski, 'O rzezbach E. E. Geflowskiego', *Wiadomości* (London, 3 Feb. 1974); 'Wnuczka rzeźbiarza E. E. Geflowskiego', *Dziennik Polski* (London, 25 July 1975); 'O Polak-ach w dziennikach Gladstona', ibid. (10 Sept. 1982); 'E. E. Geflowski i lord Bathurst', ibid. (29 Oct. 1984). For Geflowski's work in India see *Kurier Warszawski* (4 Aug. 1880), 4, and *Tydzień Polski* (1880), no. 33, p. 523. See also U. Thieme and F. Becker, *Allgemeines Lexikon der bildenden Künstler* xiii (1920), 335.

[44] R. L. Poole, *Catalogue of Portraits in the Pos-session of the University of Oxford* (Oxford His-torical Society), i (1912), p. 123. The bust is in the Bodleian and is illustrated by M. Paszkiewicz (see n. 43, above).

FIG. 54. The east end of the Chapel showing the reredos, as restored by Sir Gilbert Scott, and E. E. Geflowski's statuary.

FIG. 55. The east end of the Chapel, 1987, showing the retable over the altar (by C. E. Kempe, 1889)

with Scott to provide the reredos figures and in December he was entrusted by the College with the loan of its copies of an illustrated Froissart and of Meyricke's *Ancient Armour* to provide him with models.[45] Over the next four years he supplied all but one of the thirty-six statues of apostles, prelates, and Lancastrian notables and the eighty-two statuettes which are still convincing enough to mislead the unthinking into believing that they are medieval work.[46] By October 1875 the reredos and its statuary were complete (Fig. 54). But other work continued. In 1876 a credence with a stone canopy for the east end of the north wall was commissioned, and an adjoining doorway was ordered to be blocked with stone (Fig. 56). This was the doorway into the medieval vestry which had once existed to the north of the Chapel (as at New College), and which had been revealed during the restoration work. Scott had wished to reopen it and designed an outside stair approach to it (Fig. 57) which was not accepted. This doorway resurfaced during the recent (1985) refacing of the exterior of the north wall of the Chapel. It has taken cover once again but not before its history has been traced by Mr Nicholas Doggett.[47]

After the spring of 1877 the only references to the Chapel in the records relate to its windows and to its sundial. Subscribers to the Gothic screen had allowed their subscriptions to be diverted to the cost of replacing the glass in the windows in the chancel. The replacements were ordered from Clayton and Bell and were installed between the autumn of 1877 and June 1879. They are not unworthy companions for the fifteenth-century antechapel windows and for the large west window by Hardman of Birmingham, which had been ordered in 1861 as a memorial to Warden Sneyd.[48]

The story of the sundial is a less happy one. The original, designed by Christopher Wren and built by William Byrd, had been placed by Wren in 1659 between the pinnacles in the centre bay of the south wall of the Chapel.[49] There it was an elegant foil to the gate-tower opposite, and was also conveniently placed for the Oxford watchmakers whom Mr Rowell in the 1870s could remember setting their watches by it.[50]

[45] MS 401(f), 17 Dec. 1873.

[46] *The Builder* (3 May 1879), 489 attributes the unidentified exception to the admiral-sculptor Count Gleichen and credits the 'architectural sculpture' to Henry Terry — evidently an outstandingly gifted craftsman. The full-page illustration of the reredos (ibid., p. 485 and our Fig. 54) shows the altar in its original state and before it acquired the retable by C. E. Kempe which H. O. Wakeman presented to the Chapel in 1889 (see Fig. 55).

[47] *Oxoniensia*, xlix (1984), 277–87.

[48] MS 401(f), 21 May 1861; F. E. Hutchinson,

Medieval Glass at All Souls College (1949), p. 16.

[49] The Bursars' Roll for 1658–9 (when Wren was one of the bursars) records the payment of £34. 11s. 6d. in all to 'Byrd' for 'worke about the Diall', and also a payment to 'M. Hawkins' of £16. 10s. for painting it. Robert Plot (*Natural History of Oxford-shire* (1677), p. 289) attributes the design of the sundial to Wren and praises its accuracy. For Byrd see J. C. Cole, 'William Byrd, Stonecutter and Mason', *Oxoniensia* xiv (1949), 63–74.

[50] Burrows, *Worthies*, p. 233.

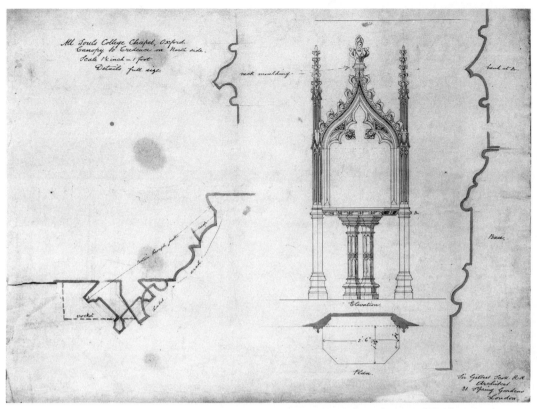

FIG. 56. The credence in the north wall at the east end of the Chapel (1876) removed to make way for Sir William Anson's monument in 1918. *Drawing by Sir Gilbert Scott.* *British Architectural Library*

In August 1871 the sundial was reported to be so much out of repair (Fig. 58) that it had to be removed (at a cost of £23. 16s. 7d.). In December 1874 a proposal that after repair it be returned to its original position was lost, and in May 1877 it was decided (in spite of the future Warden Anson's opposition) to place it over the centre of the south front of the Codrington Library. And there it remains, a splendid and disproportionate anachronism, breaking Hawksmoor's uninterrupted roof-line, gratuitously destroying the perfect symmetry of his North Quadrangle, and leaving the answering cartouche of arms which he had set over the south front of the Hall, unbalanced.

The end of the 1870s saw not only the end of the Chapel restoration but also a development that was symbolic of the changing ethos of the College. It concerned the Old Library, which had been partitioned in 1751 for occupation by Robert Vansittart. Later, it would seem that the room was accommodating two fellows, and by 1878 part of it was already being used as a lecture room — an indication of the increased academic interests of a College which was then only six years short of electing its first research fellow. In

PLAN.

FIG. 57. The Chapel: unexecuted project for an outside stair giving access to a blocked doorway uncovered during restoration work in 1876. This was in the north wall towards the east end and originally had given access to an external vestry demolished in the eighteenth century. *Drawing by Sir Gilbert Scott. All Souls Archives*

June 1879 Robarts placed his rooms at the disposal of the College, the Domestic Bursar to have the 'ceiling and partitions' removed for its ultimate fitting-up as a lecture room. This can only have been the other half of the Old Library, and though Robarts added a characteristic rider — that the work was to be done when 'convenient' to himself — in 1884 the work *was* done, and as a result it has been possible for Chichele Lectures to be delivered in a room whose academic pedigree begins in the 1440s.

* * *

Fig. 58. The south front of the Chapel showing Wren's sundial of 1659 in its original position. It was removed in Aug. 1871 and re-erected over the centre of the south front of the Codrington Library in 1877. *Photograph, c. 1870. Bodleian Library*

A few words in conclusion. Just as 1750 saw the end of 'Hawksmoring and Townsending' so 1880 saw the end of 'Cluttoning and Scotting'. No substantial new buildings were erected on the College site until the Visiting Fellows' studies were built by the Oxford Architects' Partnership nearly a century later, in the 1960s. These are an excellent example of what can be done if one accepts the principle that Hawksmoor had adopted two hundred and fifty years earlier, i.e. that new functions should be accommodated in buildings whose exteriors show respect for their senior neighbours. That is *not* to say that there were no ambitious plans for less respectful additions to the College in the 1930s — as readers of Dr Colvin's *Unbuilt Oxford* know; nor that no attention was paid to the conservation of our heritage — in the 1960s and 1970s the twin towers and the whole of the exterior of the south and west ranges of the College were restored; and the 1980s have been, are being, and will be devoted to the interior ranges of the Front and North Quadrangles. Nobody who has been in College during that period can honestly echo the lines written in another context by our quondam fellow, Bishop Heber:

No workman steel, no ponderous axes rung;
Like some tall palm the noiseless fabric sprung.
Majestic silence! . . .[51]

But it has been worth it: All Souls should be able to face the future in first-class architectural condition.

---

[51] R. Heber, *Palestine: A Prize-Poem, Recited in the Theatre, Oxford, June 15, 1803*, p. 16. The lines — perhaps the best known of any in the poem — were composed impromptu by Heber in reaction to a remark by Walter Scott pointing out that the poem contained no reference to either the silence or the absence of tools during the construction of the Temple in Jerusalem (A. Heber, *Life of Reginald Heber*, i (1830), p. 30; J. G. Lockhart, *Life of Sir Walter Scott*, ii (Edinburgh, 1902), p. 106).

E. H. NEW'S NEW LOGGAN VIEW, 1923 (Fig. 59)

PLAN, 1987 (Fig. 60)

APPENDICES A—C

INDEX

FIG. 59. A bird's-eye view of All Souls College from the south by E. H. New, 1923, drawn for New's *New Loggan Guide to Oxford Colleges* (1932). *Ashmolean Museum, Oxford*

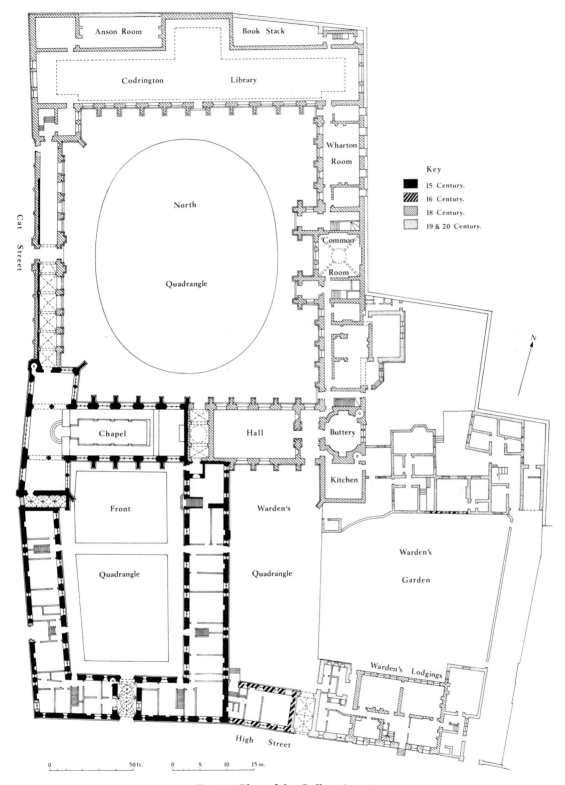

FIG. 60. Plan of the College in 1987

(77)

APPENDIX A

Building at All Souls, 1553–1751

Selected Entries from the Warden's Register (Warden's MS 3) and the College Benefactors' Book

[fo. 11ᵛ] Here folowethe the names of suche benefactours as dyd contribute any money towardes the buyldynng up and finysshyng of the lodgyngs upon the backe syde of the college from the square of the same college weste unto a voyd place east, and fruntyng along by the hyghe streat sowthe, the whyche lodgyngs were fynysshed in the yere of our lord god MCCCCCLIII.[1]

all somtyme felows of the college.

Fyrst	Syr William Peter knyght somtyme felowe of the college dyd gyve in moneye	v li.
Item	Syr John Mason knyght somtyme felowe of the college	iiijli.
Item	Rychard Bartlet esquyer doctor of physike	xxs.
Item	David Poole doctor of lawe	xls.
Item	Wylliam Cooke doctor of lawe	xls.
Item	John Pope bacheler of lawe	xls.
Item	Rycharde Lyelle doctor of lawe	xxs.
Item	John Gybon doctor of lawe	xxs.
Item	John Fuller doctor of lawe	xxs.
Item	Gylbert Boorne master of arte	xxs.
Item	Roger Stokeley master of arte somtyme Warden	xls.
Item	Nicolas Bullyngham bacheler of lawe	xxvjs.viijd
Item	Edward Napper master of arte	xxs.
Item	John Warner doctor of physike and Warden of the College at the same tyme and the setter on of the sayd woorke and the gatherer of the sayd sommes and the mover and perswader of the sayd persons to gyve the money, dyd gyve out of hys own purse in money.	x li.
Item	the sayd John Warner havyng money in hys hands to bestowe to good and charitable uses dyd gyve therof	ls.

Summa xxxvj li. xvjs. viijd.

---

[1] This records the extension of the College's street frontage eastwards in 1553 (see Fig. 4).

Item the sayd John Warner havyng in hys hands of the college's money at the decayng of money to the halfe valore at two cryes forty pounds,[2] payd the same somme wholly towards the sayd buyldynng beryng the losse of the same fall hym self   xx li.

Item he gave tymber and dyverse other thyngs.

[fo. 12]   The Warden's Garden

The Warden's garden was sometymes the Rose Inne,[3] and being purcha[sed] by Sir William Peter knight, and geven to the colledg it laye wast and out of order, untill the yere of our Lorde 1573 when Mr. Robert Hovenden Warden seing it convenient for a garden roome and no use thereof as it laye, desired the companye to graunt it him, and he woulde inclose it for a garden purposing to impale it, and to remove the well which was called the Rose well, standing in it (whereof it was saide merelie the fellowes of Allsoln colledg wasshed everie daye in rose water) uppon his owne charges. But after seing the palinge woulde be to litle purpose, and the walinge verie chargable, he required the companie to geve him the reversion of a lease in Wedon Weston ... rented at xxs. yerelie: to be solde, and the mony imploied in the walling, and what soever the cost amounted above, the Warden to beare it. This was graunted and the lease made unto one George Smithe Master of Art and fellow. The weeke before Easter in Anno 1574 he beganne to levell the ground, in digging whereof where found in old foundacions as many stoanes as built the wall except xl[ti] loades onelie, fetched from the quarrye; ther were supposed to be CC loades. The whole charge of the walle besides this stoane withe leveling the ground came to xiiij li. ijs. xd. And the well with the plompe[4] xls.

By me R. Hovenden

Note the peece of wall conteining xvj perches on the foundacione, which is betwene the Warden's garden and Magdalen colledg ground from the thatched house northwarde, is part of Magdalen colledg fence there standing some tyme an pale answearable to the rest: it was builded 4 August 1576. The Warden giving the stuf and Hughe Burton tenant to Magdalen Colledg paying the workeman, the charges in all: xlixs. vijd.

R. Hovenden

---

[2] At this time the value of English money was seriously affected by debasement and a falling rate of exchange.

[3] The Rose Inn occupied some or all of the site of the former Bedel Hall (no. 7 in Fig. 1). This had been acquired by All Souls in 1531/2, subject to a quit-rent of 18s., and it was this quit-rent that Sir William Petre gave to the College in 1557/8 (H. E. Salter, *Survey of Oxford*, i, ed. W. A. Pantin (Oxford Historical Society, 1960), pp. 134–5).

[4] Pump.

[fo. 12]   Chaplens chambers

The pece of bulding conteyning 4. chambers towe above and two beneth where the
Chaplens are now lodged, abutting on the closter south, and on Catstreate west,[5]
was as it is said, purposed to builde a steeple uppon at the beginning; but it was a
stoarehouse unto the yere of our lorde 1570, when the Archbisshop Matthu Parker
meanyng to convert the Coristers roomes into schollerships, to be elected out of
Canterberie Schole, caused Doctor Barber then Warden, and the companie to builde
that lodging, that roome might be in the quadrangle for the schollers. So was it
begonne Anno domini 1571 in D. Barber's tyme, but being left of by reason of the
plague, was ended Anno 1572. Mr. Hovenden then Warden. And touching the
schollerships nothing done at the writing hereof 1574. Junij 23. nor is like here after,
the Archbisshop being deade who departed the 18 of Maij. 1575.

                                                                    R. Hovenden

[fo. 76] *Reparations and provisions of our College in the later tyme of Dr. Hovenden*
Warden, from the yeare 1593, until 1613.

1594   The faire stone Woodhouse at the end of the Warden's garden was builded
        this yeare.[6]
1596   The Kitchen, the passage afore the Kitchen, and Stafford Lane,[7] were nowe
        all first paved with ragge.
1598   Our Librarye, newly vaulted with plaister of Paris and furnished with new
        deskes.[8]
1606   The Warden's studdye builded, and the rome under fitted for a kitchen
1611   The Cloister Greene, then converted into a Garden with Arbours.

Reparations and provisions, for our Colledge, in the tyme of Dr. Mocket Warden, from the
yeare 1614, until 1618.

1616   The Quadrangle paved with ragge, the lead spoutes in the Quadrangle,
        drawne pendent downe to the grownd.
1616   The Butler, who now hath his Chamber designed over the cocke, and conduite
        in the stone-woodhouse, formerlye had a lower chamber in the Quadrangle
        under our Foundre's Armes with supporters towards St. Maries.
1617   The water-cocke, and conduite under the Buttler's windowe whose springe
        head is at Comner,[9] was now erected.

---

[5] This building can be seen in the *Typus* (*front-ispiece*) at the top.
[6] See the *Typus*. Part of the south wall of this building survives (see plan, Fig. 60).
[7] The passageway beneath the Old Library leading from the Front Quadrangle to the War-den's Quadrangle was formerly known as 'Stafford's Lane', presumably after Archbishop Stafford (1443–52). The mouldings of its two doorways were destroyed when the passage was widened in 1758 (*Victoria County History of Oxford-shire*, iii. 186).
[8] For the refitting of the Library in 1598 see B. H. Streeter, *The Chained Library* (1931), pp. 171–82.
[9] Cumnor, three miles south-west of Oxford.

[fo. 76ᵛ]   *Reparations and provisions for our Colledge in the tyme of Dr. Astley Warden.*

1618   The new Parler in the Lodginge made into one roome and furnished, which formerly was 3 homly roomes, one an old kitchen, a larder and a roome for poultrye.

1618   The highe table in the Colledge Halle made a new with a coople of Drawers to inlardge it.

1619   The murrey velvet carpet, with gold and silke frenge, for the Communion Table in the Chappell was then bought by the Colledge.

1619   The Inner Buttery floaer, taken lower, for givinge better roome for Barrells.

1621   The foundation stones rownd about our Colledge, beinge much consumed and demolished, were nowe firmly repayred and supplyed.[10]

1622   The streete on the Colledge two sides, towardes the streete, were now paved with peeble.

1623   The little peeble Courte at the entrance into the Warden's garden, was then paved with peeble and seates then made first about the same.

[fo. 78]

1629   The Communion Table in the Chappell was advanced from the middle of the Chancell to the upper end above the ascendinge stepps.

1629   The pavement in the Warden's Parlour closet was first layd with a voydinge chanell into the streete.

1630   The Carfox Conduite water was conveyed out from the streete into the sayd closet by pype and cocke.[11]

1630   Our Colledge Inner Seller was inlarged in length shootinge alonge betweene the Chapell and the Cloystere.

1633   This yeare our Colledge gats were repaired, and lyned face-way towards the streete, and lykwise newly adornde with the Armes of his Majestie, of our Prince, and of our founder;[12] And allsoe the three statues over our gates of our Saviour, of Kinge Henry the sixt, and our founder, were at the same tyme polished, smothed, and renewed, with vernishe, and guilt, as formerly they had beene.

[fo. 79ᵛ]

1703   About this time several Letters came from Mr. George Clark Fellow of the College wherein he desires leave to build himself Lodgings in the College for his owne life, and then to come to the use of the College for ever; to which the College readyly consent; and in prospect likewise of future Benefactions,

[10] This presumably refers to a general repair of the plinths.

[11] A new water-supply distributed from a conduit at Carfax had recently become available.

[12] See Loggan's engraving (Fig. 3). The present gates date from the eighteenth century.

they begin in July to pull down the old Cloysters of four sides, and build one onely Cloyster; leaving the rest of the Ground for Mr. Clark to erect his Building upon.

B.G[ardiner], W[arden]

With some of the rough stones of the Cloysters, the Society agree to build a wall of fourteen foot high between the Warden's Garden and the House belonging to Magalen College att this time in possession of Henry White, Alderman; he contributing a share towards it, as is at large expressd in certain Articles bearing date Aug.4.1703 between the College and the said H. White. One part of which Articles remain in the Bursary

B.G.W.

Note. There is nothing said in these Articles to prejudice the privilege wee enjoy by prescription of 109 years of having the Warden's stone-woodhouse att the end of the Garden to stand, as it does, in the upper end of the wall. Vide pag.76 hujusce libri.

B.G.W.

1704   The beginning of this year, the College purchast an old house, adjoyning to the Warden's Lodgings, of Joanna Fry, widow, with the summ of £190, £10 more being given to the Tenant for his removal before his lease was expir'd. This £200 was the free gift of Ralph Snow Esqr. who now was, and had long been Treasurer of the Houshold att the Palace of Lambeth, namely to his Grace Gilbert Sheldon of ever honour'd memory (to whom he was a Servant when Warden of this College) to Arch Bishops Sancroft, Tillotson, and Tenison.

[fo. 80]

1706   Upon the ground where this old house stood (together with a piece of the Warden's Garden allowed to Mr. Clarke) he, i.e. Dr. Clarke, chooses to build his Lodgings rather than in the Grove where he att first designed them; and they being began in April 1704 were finished and inhabited about April 1706. The conditions between the Warden and College and Mr. Clarke are to be seen in the Leiger Book. God send us more such ample Benefactours.

Att the same time, att the College expence, namely from money rising from some Gawdies, and other entertainments which were now layd aside for this use, was built that single Pile of two windows in breadth (joyning the Old Lodgings to Mr. Clarke's new ones) which fell to the present use of me.

B.G. Warden

1710   April 7. dyed General Christopher Codrington: who left the College by will
        £10000 for a library etc.

1714   In this year George Clarke abovementioned (now Dr. of Laws) Fellow of the
        College, put up att his own expense entirely, that Noble Ornament of Marble
        att the East End, and North and South sides, of the Chappell near the
        Communion Table;[13] giving likewise with that the Rich Crimson Velvet
        Furniture, lac'd and fringd with Gold. By Christmas Day 1714 this Noble
        Benefaction was completely finished. The Purple Velvet Communion Table-
        Cloth, which I had given in the first year of my Warden ship, was sold for
        Cushions for the University Church.

1715   In this year was began (and finished before Easter 1716) the Painting att the East
        End of the Chappell over the Marble, done by Mr. Thornhill.[14] For this work
        Henry Seymour-Portman Esq'. (Heir to Sir William Portman Baronett a for-
        mer Benefactour to our College) gave £200: Mr. John Webb late Fellow, £20.

[fo. 80ᵛ]

1716   This year in the Spring, the roof of the Inner Chappell was richly adorn'd
        with gilded roses and network, being done upon canvass sett in frames: and
        also the sides painted and adorn'd with figures, all by the hand of Mr. James
        Thornhill aforesaid, att the expence of the Honourable Dodington Grevile
        Esq'. (uncle to the present Lord Brooke) now a Fellow of this College. Itt
        cost him £262 10s.
                Mem: The alteration of the skreen, and other ornaments in the
        Outward Chapell was done att the expence of the College; with moneys savd
        from Gawdies, Sconces etc.

1718   The beginning of this year, the Societye intending to make some additional
        buildings in the Back Quadrangle, answerable to the Codrington Library,
        they acquainted their Friends with the Design, who contributed as follows,
        viz. Earl of Carnarvon £200. Dr. Henry Godolphin £100. Dr. Rob. Wood
        £100. Mr. John Aldworth £100. Dr. Thomas Tanner, Chancellor of
        Norwich £50. Mr. Roger Williams £31 10s. Sir John Shadwell £21. The
        Rev. Mr. Peter Waldoe £20. Mr. Robert Lloyd £20. The Rev. Mr. Francis
        Offley £10 10s. The Rev. Mr. Marshal Bridges £10 10s.[15] Sir Nathanael
        Lloyd gave the income of his Fellowship, for so long as he shou'd continue
        Fellow: the first payment to be made for the year 1719. Dr. Philip Code gave a
        legacy of £50, but on such conditions as in the end made it come but to £36.

---

[13] Several designs for this altar-piece, some of them by Hawksmoor, are among Dr Clarke's drawings at Worcester College (see H. M. Colvin, *A Catalogue of Architectural Drawings of the Eighteenth and Nineteenth Centuries in the Library of Worcester College, Oxford* (1964), p. 55).

[14] For this see Fig. 39 and *Victoria County History of Oxfordshire*, iii. 184.

[15] These were all former fellows of the College with the exception of the Earl of Carnarvon and Peter Waldoe, who was a former Chaplain.

1720 The Right Honourable Henry Lord Carlton gave £100. The Honourable General William Steuart, to finish the Northern Tower, and the staircase in it, gave £786. The Honourable and Reverend Dr. Richard Hill Fellow of Eaton College several times employed as a Publick Minister by their Majesties King William and Queen Anne, gave £50. Thomas Palmer of Fairfield in Somersettshire Esqr. Burgess for Bridgwater, gave £50. The most noble Philip Duke of Wharton for building the Pile which joyns the Codrington Library to the Northern (or Steuart's) Tower contracted with the Builders for £1183:00:00.

[fo. 81]

1724 Sir Nathanael Lloyd gave his Buildings upon conditions to be seen in an Order of the House dated March 3^d 1723/4, and Bonds in the Leiger-Booke about the same date. It cost him something above £1200 besides £142 11s.06d. which was the product of his Fellowship for 4 years and a half, which he had formerly given to the College and which he now desir'd might be added to his Building: and was so done.

1727 Sr Peter Mews Chancellour of the Diocese of Winchester and formerly fellow of the College bequeathed by will the summe of one hundred Pounds to be laid out upon the buildings then erecting or to be erected: in observance of which clause the College agreed to build that part of the Cloysters that from the Gate joyns the Library, the expense of which amounted exactly to the summe of £100.

[The Wardens' record of gifts towards the cost of building ends at this point, but the *Benefactors' Book* includes (in Latin) further relevant donations as follows:]

1729 To build the new Hall, Buttery and Kitchen: Dr. Piers Dod, M.D., of St. Bartholomew's Hospital, London, £200; Richard Willis, Bishop of Winchester, £100; the Hon. Thomas, Lord Trevor of Bromham, £100; the Hon. Charles, Lord Talbot of Hensol, Lord Chancellor, £100; the Hon. Dodington Grevile, £100; the Rev. Thomas Tanner, Bishop of St. Asaph, £50; the Hon. William, Lord Digby, £50; the Hon. Wriothesley Digby, Ll.D., Fellow of All Souls, £50; Charles Delafaye, Esqr. Secretary to the Duke of Newcastle, 50 guineas; Timothy Geers, formerly Fellow of All Souls, 5 guineas. The Warden and College expended £1331 1s. 1d. for the same purpose, in addition to £600 paid to Sir Nathaniel Lloyd for the interest on £1000 received from him as a loan.

1733 The Hon. Dodington Grevile gave £750 to complete the gateway on the west side of the North Quadrangle together with the Cloister between the Chapel and the said gateway on condition that he should be paid £30 annually by the College.

Dr. George Clarke lined the walls of the Hall with wainscot (*opere tabulato*) and made the marble chimney-piece (*tabulam focariam marmore ornatam*) at his own expense.

1740   Sir Nathaniel Lloyd bequeathed £1000 to complete the Codrington Library or the adjoining buildings in the North Quadrangle.

1748   Eight Fellows gave a total of £34 18s. owed to them by the College towards the cost of renewing the paving in the Old Quadrangle.

1751   The Hon. Wriothesley Digby gave £50 towards the cost of renewing the pavement in the Old Quadrangle.

APPENDIX B

Hawksmoor's Letter to Dr George Clarke, dated 17 February 1714/15[1]

S^r

The Explanation of the Designes for All Souls

I send you, as followeth vizt.

No. 1. Is the plann generall of the whole designe, which may be altered in some particulars of the measures (to make it answer the ground) without changeing the essentiall parts of the fabricks.*

The irregularity of the Chapell will occasion some disagreement in the front towards the Piazza[2] by its not being at right angles, but that may be dispens'd withall, since (in all appearance) it will seem uniform.

The Vestibule, or middle passage that lyes between the Hall and the end of the Chapell serves only for communication from the Old Quadrangle to the New one, unless you will leave 2 dores into the Hall, which may be easyly fill'd up, if not found usefull. But if you shou'd make the entrance of the Hall at this end from this Vestibule and place the screen here, you woud save roome and add to the length of the Hall considerably, however I have (according to your hints) prepar'd the entrance and screen at the other end next the Buttry. The chimney in the Hall I wou'd place in the side wall, rather than in the middle of the floor. I propose the Vestibule afforsay'd to be vaulted and to rise from the paveing to the vault as high as the Hall ceiling, and above the leads of the Hall and Chapell to rise still 15 foot higher to forme an oblong turret† for the service of the Chapell bell, and to break the long extent of this wing, more agreeably. The Hall, shou'd be all vaulted underneath, to preserve the paving, wainscots etc. and to make it more wholsome.

The proposition of the Kitchen and Offices is done 2 severall ways as you may see in the plan of the (Dormitory) next New College and I am of opinion, that, what I have put in that plan, is better, than the proposall in the generall plan for them Offices.

The Great Dormitory, and Common Room is much after your owne direction, however you may in some of the particulars change it without destroying the main

---

* *Marginal note in Dr Clarke's hand*: This, to be followed.

† *Marginal note*: I hope the College will not build this oblong Turret, which will be expensive, and I fear, look very heavy GC.

---

[1] Abbreviations have been expanded in this transcription of the text and the erratic capitalization of the original has been to some extent regularized.

[2] The future Radcliffe Square.

intention. This should all be vaulted in the cellars and the Common Roome both under foot and over head, the stairs made of hard stone and 2 thick party walls, next the Hall at one end and the Library at the other riseing 6 foot higher than the roofs and leads, to keep any accident of fire from consuming all at once.

The Library has it's entrance in the middle, which is distinguish'd within, by a large recess breaking toward Hart Hall,[3] and contain'd under the suffite of a large Gothick arch which is humour'd by 2 other arches of the like nature on the right hand and left which all together circumscribe this middle part or center of the Library. Over these arches rises a turret‡ (as high as that on the Chapell side) with windows striking downe into the room placed in form of a Gothick lantern.

The 2 extream ends of the Library are vary'd by 2 other of the sayd Gothick arches, for the better ornament both of the walls and ceilings, but note that their suffites neither lessen the room, nor hinder the view. The manner of the ceiling I wou'd propose to be wainscot work divided into pannells, (cum cistellis rosarum deaurat.)[4]

The places for archives,[5] and studys with chimnys are separated by strong party walls, pierced with lesser arches whose overtures may be usefull for bookes, etc.[6] The stairs and other conveniencys are all (I hope) according to your minde, in generall, altho not in every little part. I must desire, cellars vaulted, under the whole Library, other wayes the books will suffer much. The studys, and archives ought also to be vaulted with brick in every story. vid.ᵉ the example of the Vatican Library.

I have designed a Portico and Gate (next the Great Piazza) after the Roman Order, to shew that we are not quite out of charity with that manner of building.

The plann mark[ed] N° 2 is the designe of the Great Dormitory and Common Room with the parts adjoyning.

N° 3 is the Entry or Vestbulum between the Hall and Chapell. and the same will be in appearance on the wing of the Library.[7]

N° 4 shews the front of the Old Quadrangle to the High-Street with an additionall storye, and the windows somwhat alterd.

N° 5 a bay of the Old Building at large with the manner of chassing (if required).

N° 6 is a generall perspective of the Chapell, Library, and Great Dormitory, with a part of the Old Quadrangle alter'd.

I have also sent two scetches of rebuilding, after the Antique, keeping the Hall and Chapell Gothick only.[8]

‡ *Marginal note*: I hope the College will not build this Turret GC.

---

[3] Now Hertford College.

[4] 'With compartments of gilded roses'.

[5] By 'archives' Hawksmoor probably means lockable cupboards, as in the Bodleian Library.

[6] Hawksmoor's Plan no. 2 (Bodleian, MS Gough Plans 8) shows that the studies were the two rooms opening off the Library on the north side at each end, as shown in Fig. 23. They are separated from the Library proper by walls con-

taining recesses such as Hawksmoor describes.

[7] This presumably means that it is aligned with the central projection of the Library.

[8] Two drawings at Worcester College dated 1714 show such a scheme (Colvin, *A Catalogue of Architectural Drawings of the Eighteenth and Nineteenth Centuries in the Library of Worcester College, Oxford* (1964), pls. 69, 70).

I must ask leave to say somthing in favour of the Old Quadrangle, built by your most Reverend Founder, for altho it may have some faults yet it is not without its virtues. This building is strong and durable, much more firm than any of your new buildings because they have not the substance nor workmanship, and I am confident that much conveniency and beauty, may be added to it, whereas utterly destroying or barbarously altering or mangleing it, wou'd be useing the Founder cruelly, and a loss to the present possessours.

I have offered at keeping the old walls as entire as I can, only putting in some windows carefully or perhaps enlargeing others, as necessity may require, but I wou'd open as little toward the street as is possible. I have added upon paper an upper story in form of a perpetuall arcade of the Gothick manner that may be open or sollid as oft as needfull, and which will strike in, with those small irregularitys frequent in the Gothick workes, and alltogether, preserve a reasonable uniformity; my intentions you may see by the drawings, more fully, and if I am not quite right in my notion, yet I am certain if I may be assisted with your thoughts in this affair it will improve the thing beyond contradiction. Vid. N° 3.

Whatever is good in its kinde ought to be preserv'd in respect to antiquity, as well as our present advantage, for destruction can be profitable to none but such as live by it.

N° V. I have made a drawing (pretty large) of a bay of the Old Building next the High Street which may serve as a specimen in many other cases, to put the workmen in minde how to place a chass[9] window in a front of a Gothick building, without destroying the strength of the fabrick, and the order and beauty of the compartment.

To doe this, it is of absolute necessity to keep the stone arch over the head of the window, or if it must be destroyed by enlargeing the window; supply it with a new one.

Never suffer the outward moldings on the jaumbs of the windows and suffite, to be cut away, for that takes off all the ornament and strength of the designe.

The more the chasse frame of wood, and chass stands from the out face of the wall, it is the better because the wooden worke is defended from the rain and more strongly fix'd, besides the beauty it gives the overture by receding.

You may see the scandalous effect that chass windows have, by putting them flush (as workmen call it) to the outside of the wall; in the quadrangle of New College, and most other places in Oxford, and at Trinity in Cambridge most shamfully.

It is fancy'd by most of the workmen and many others that the placeing a window of chass; to the very outside of the wall, gains more light, than when it receds, as the windows doe in the Banqueting House, and all Italian and Gothick buildings. But this I positivly declare a mistake, for the glass being a diaphanous plain, or rather an invisible septum to keep out the weather it is noe matter in what part of the wall you place it, whether outside, inside, or middle.

What I am offering at in this article is for the preservation of antient durable

---

[9] Sash.

publick buildings, that are strong and usfull, instead of erecting new fantasticall perishable trash, or altering and wounding the old by unskillful knavish workmen and this leads me to say somthing further by way of encouragement towards generall design and proper forcast in this affair architectionicall that may regard both old and new erections.

When London was burnt in 1666. out of that fatall accidentall mischief one might have expected some good when the Phenix was to rise again, viz.ᵗ a convenient regular well built citty, excellent, skillfull, honest artificers made by the greatness and quantity of the worke in rebuilding such a capital. but instead of these, we have noe city, nor streets, nor houses, but a chaos of dirty rotten sheds, allways tumbling or takeing fire, with winding crooked passages (scarse practicable) lakes of mud and rills of stinking mire running through them.

The workmen [are] soe far from skill or honesty that the generall part of 'em are more brutall and stupid then, in the remotest part of Britain and the longer they worke the worse they grow, as you may see in all the additional scoundrell streets they are continually cobling up, to sell by wholesale and this is not all in London, for this sort of vermin has run and spread all over the country, and as they have ruined the capitall soe have they all the other citys and townes in England more or less, together with working the destruction of many a good old mansion house and durable castle etc. Soe that it is a question which was the worse calamity the burning, or rebuilding by these villains, for the first was quick and soon over, the later slow but perpetuall.

It is not quite fair to lay all the blame, of the above mention'd misfortunes upon those poor reptiles for it is very astonishing that the Government, and Legislature wou'd not enter into this affair most strenuously and effectually at such a time when they had so favourable an opportunity to rebuild London the most august towne in the world, and either have keept it to its old dimention, or if it was reasonable to let it swell to a larger, they ought for the publick good to have guided it into a regular and commodious form, and not have suffered it to run into an ugly inconvenient self destroying unweildy monster. These I say one might have wished for from the powers above sayd, and many other publick benefits of like nature, but when we may entertain any hopes of seeing any such performed by them God only knows.

Now to apply this argument by looking back we see the misfortunes of London in rebuilding as well as augmenting it, by not haveing generall draughts, and regular schemes, and what irreparable inconvenience and mischief has bin produced, let us returne to Oxford and looke forward upon the hopes we may have in the Universitys of doing as much good as we can and avoyding the ills that may hapen by omiting a little previous care.

It cannot therfore be improper to lay downe such draughts and designes for repairing the old and erecting new fabricks for the embellishment, and use of the University as may in time come to perfection altho not soe quickly as we might wish, for when we survey what we have done, beyond expectation and if we consider the noble benefactions given and the genius that now seems to govern we need not dispair of, accomplishing any thing that may render this seat of the Muses admired at home and renowned abroad, but running on without any rule and well digested designes will produce nothing but chaos and tumult.

I am much delighted with your proposall for the Piazza and Library next the Schools[10] and more particularly that you have still further hopes of other enlargments you [need] but give me your hints relating to things of this nature and I will do all I can to forward them and (as I have bin pleading) will make designes for all that can be thought necessary to the use and ornament of the University.

I am always extreamly satisfyed when I can be any ways usfull to the University and when the gentlemen of that learned body express themselves pleasd with any of my endeavours, it is the highest obligation to me.

S^r I remain your most obliged humble servant

N. Hawksmoor

I beg you will present my most humble service to S^r W^m. Gifford,[11] and be pleased to tell him, that it was not any disregard to him that I did not wait on him, but the misfortune of my being out of towne.

February 17 1714/15

Westminster

[10] The future Radcliffe Library and Square. Dr John Radcliffe had died in 1714, leaving funds for the purpose of building a library in the area between St Mary's Church and the Schools Quadrangle.

[11] The first Governor of Greenwich Hospital, where Hawksmoor held the post of Clerk of Works.

APPENDIX C

The Chichele Lectures, 1912–1988

THE list of Chichele Lectures in this Appendix begins with H. A. L. Fisher's course delivered in 1912, but the idea that All Souls might sponsor independent courses of academic lectures first seems to have arisen some forty years earlier, in 1873. In one sense, indeed, 'Chichele Lectures' had in 1873 already been given for a dozen years or so. By agreement with the Executive Commissioners following on the 1850 Commission, All Souls had suppressed ten fellowships in order to fund the two 'Chichele' Professorships of Law and Diplomacy (1859) and of Modern History (1862) — and Mountague Bernard and Montagu Burrows, the respective original holders of the two chairs, certainly delivered courses of 'Chichele' lectures.

The establishment of the Chichele chairs was an example of the application of All Souls' revenues to academic purposes with the general benefit of the University in mind. In the 1870s discussion within the College of its role in the Oxford academic system was continuous and sufficiently wide (and wild) as to include consideration of the admission of undergraduates, acceptance of candidates for the Indian Civil Service, and even union with the Bodleian. It is in this context that we must see a proposal made to the College Meeting on 17 December 1873 by T. R. Buchanan (1846–1911). Buchanan was an enlightened, generous, and bibliophile fellow of the College to whom the Codrington owes much, and whose career was to culminate in the Under-Secretaryship for India in 1908. His proposal was that the College should invite 'some distinguished Foreign Professor . . . or person eminent in historical or literary enquiry' to deliver courses of lectures. He set his sights high, instancing Mommsen, Pauli, Ranke, Taine, Matthew Arnold, and John Morley as potential lecturers.

Sadly, Buchanan's imaginative proposal was withdrawn in favour of Max Müller's suggestion that Goldwin Smith be invited to deliver a single course of lectures, and it was not until 1909, when the College's standing in academic matters was unquestioned, that it was proposed at a College Meeting on 1 June, that All Souls should set aside £300 for three 'Chichele Lectureships in foreign history on the lines of the Ford's Lectureship'. The proposal was approved and evidently judged to be a success, as four courses of Chichele Lectures were given during the three years from 1912 to 1914 and a fifth course (by G. W. Prothero) was approved for 1915, though the lectures were not delivered until 1920.

On 9 June 1919 the College moved with the times in approving the appointment of a 'Chichele Lecturer or Lecturers' to lecture on law, history, political theory, or economics on the lines of and in addition to the 'Chichele Foreign History Lectureship'. These broader terms of reference seem to have commended themselves to the College, for they appear in the 1925 statutes in which there is no longer any reference to 'foreign history'. None the less, the lectureships lay dormant during the 1920s only to be revised (on a commendably charitable interpretation) to provide support for two German *émigré* scholars in 1933.

Since 1947 the Chichele Lectures have been delivered every year or every other year normally in the Old Library at All Souls. A glance at the list which follows shows that the courses have provided contrasts in both subject-matter and style: in one year the lecturer read to a select audience the galley proofs of a book which he had in the press at the time. On another occasion the normal Old Library lecture room proved quite inadequate, and Field Marshal Lord Montgomery held forth in a crowded Sheldonian Theatre. And, finally, three recent series of lectures have been innovatory in breaking with the tradition of inviting a single lecturer to give a course of lectures: they have involved several lecturers addressing themselves to a common theme in very disparate fields of knowledge.

1912	H. A. L. Fisher	The Napoleonic Influence in Europe
1912	H. Pirenne	Les Phases principales du développement politique, économique, et social en Belgique
11913	H. W. C. Davis	The Age of Gregory VII
1914	G. Baskerville	The Age of Boniface VIII
1920	G. W. Prothero	The Second Empire and the Rise of Germany
1933	E. Cassirer	Die Philosophie des Rechts
1933	J. Marschak	Quantitative Methods in Economics
1947	B. Ohlin	Some Problems in Monetary Theory and Policy
1948	A. J. Toynbee	Recurrence and Uniqueness in History
1949	J. Dover Wilson	Shakespeare and the Wars of the Roses
1950	E. M. Earle	The American Stake in Europe, 1900–1950
1951	F. Chabod	Some Aspects of Italian Foreign Policy, 1870–1919
1952	R. H. Gabriel	Jefferson; Emerson; Thoreau; William James; Melville
1953	H. Nicolson	The Evolution of Diplomatic Method
1954	E. Wind	Art and Scholarship under Julius II

1955	C. S. Lewis	Milton
1957	A. Waley	The Opium War Seen through Chinese Eyes
1959	F.-M. Lord Montgomery	The Conflict between East and West
1960	Lord Attlee	Changes in the Conception and Structure of the British Empire during the Last Half Century
1961	E. A. Lowe	[On Palaeography]
1962	R. Hoggart	Artist, Organizations, and Audiences
1964	F. R. Leavis	Dickens: Art and Social Criticism
1964	O. Lattimore	Between the Great Wall and Siberia
1965	Lord Robbins	The Theory of Economics in the History of Economic Thought
1967	R. Birley	The British Empire in Prospect and Retrospect
1969	G. F. Kennan	The Marquis de Custine and the Russia of 1839
1970	Sir R. Harrod	Social Science, Morals, and Mystery
1971	C. Buchanan	The State of Britain
1972	R. Aron	Social Crisis and Sociology
1973	R. H. Jenkins	Patterns of Atlantic Political Leadership, 1918–1960
1975	A. Cox	The US Supreme Court in American Government
1978	C. Shannon	The Wonderful World of Feedback
1980	L. Kołakowski	The Illusions of Cultural Universalism; Is a Christian Tolerance Possible?
1982	A. Montefiore, *et al.*	The Novelist as Philosopher: Modern Fiction and the History of Ideas (Lectures by A. Montefiore, A. M. Quinton, J. Elster, J. P. Stern, and R. Scruton)
1984	C. Rycroft, *et al.*	Freud and the Humanities (Lectures by C. Rycroft, A. Starr, R. Ellmann, E. H. Gombrich, S. Dresden, F. Huxley, and H. Lloyd-Jones)
1986	H. M. Colvin and J. S. G. Simmons	All Souls: A College and its Buildings
1988	Sir A. Cairncross	Britain's Industrial Decline

INDEX

Abingdon Abbey, Berks. 5
Adderbury Church, Oxon. 16
Aichl, Jan Santini, architect 46
Aldrich, Henry, Dean of Christ Church 24
Aldworth, John 83
Anson, Sir William, Warden 47, 71

Barber, Richard, Warden 80
Bartlett, Dr Richard 78
Bathurst, 5th Earl 65, 67
Beckley Park, Oxon. 6
Benham, Samuel, architect 54
Bernard, Mountague, Prof. 70, 91
Beverley Minster, Yorks. 33
Birmingham, Oratory School 61
Blackstone, Sir William 47
Blenheim Palace, Oxon. 27
Blore, Edward, architect 61
Boorne, Gilbert 78
Branche, John, carpenter 5
Bridges, Revd. Marshall, 83
Bruton, E. G., architect 58
Buchanan, T. R. 91
Bullyngham, Nicolas 78
Burford, Oxon., quarry 5
Burrows, Montagu, Prof. 20, 64, 91
Burton, Hugh 79
Byrd, William, mason 70, 71 n.

Campbell, Colen, architect 24
Carleton ('Charlton'), Henry Boyle, 1st Baron 84
Carnarvon, 1st Earl of 33, 83
Carowe, Robert, carpenter 11 n.
Chevynton, Richard, mason 5
Chichele, Henry, Archbishop of Canterbury 1–18; statue of 6, 17
Chichele Lectures 91–4
Chichele Professors 47, 91
Clarence, Duke of 1
Clarke, Dr George 20–43 passim, 52, 81–2, 83, 85, 86
Clayton & Bell, glass-painters 70
Clifford, Richard, Bishop of London 18
Clutton, Henry, architect 61–5
Code, Dr Philip 83

Codrington, Christopher 27, 83
Cooke, Dr William 78
Croydon Palace, Surrey 8, 17
Cumnor, Berks. 6, 80

Dean, Edward 49
Delafaye, Charles 84
Digby, William, 5th Baron 84
Digby, Hon. Wriothesley 84, 85
Dod, Dr Piers 84
Doggett, Nicholas 70
Druell, John 4, 5, 8, 17

Elkyn, Thomas, mason 16
Eton College, Bucks. 8, 9, 16
Evelyn, John 58 n.
Eynsham, Oxon. 6

Finch, Hon. Leopold William, Warden 54
Fotheringhay, Northants 8
Fry, Joanna 82
Fuller, Isaac, painter 58, 63
Fuller, Dr John 78

Gardiner, B., Warden 82
Gawłowski, Emanuel Edward, sculptor 67
Geers, Timothy 84
Geflowski see Gawlowski
Gibbs, James, architect 33
Gifford, Sir William 90
Gleichen, Count, sculptor 70 n.
Godolphin, Henry, Dean of St Paul's 33, 83
Greville, Hon. Dodington 39, 83, 84, 85
Gybon, Dr John 78

Hardman, John, glass-painter 70
Hartswood Church, Surrey 60
Harvey, Michael, carver 31 n.
Hawkins, M., painter 71 n.
Hawksmoor, Nicholas, architect 19–46 passim; letter to Dr Clarke 86–90
Headington, Oxon., quarry 5
Hearne, Thomas 20

Henley-on-Thames, Oxon. 6
Henry VI 1, 9, 16; arms of 81; painting of 25; statue of 6, 17
Hill, Dr Richard 84
Horeham, Bucks. 6
Hovenden, Robert, Warden 79, 80
Hulse, Sir Edward 62
Hunting, Dr Pamela 60

Isham, Edward, Warden 47

James, John, architect 24 n.
Janyns, Robert, mason 5
Johnson, James, builder 54, 56
Johnson, Samuel 49 n.

Kempe, C. E., ecclesiastical artist 70 n.
Ker, W. P. 48
Keys, Roger, Warden 8

Lambeth Palace, Surrey 4, 8, 17
Legge, Hon. Edward, Warden 47, 52
Leighton, Francis, Warden 47, 54
Lloyd, Sir Nathaniel 31, 33, 43, 83, 84, 85
Lloyd, Robert 83
London, Banqueting House, Whitehall 89; Great Fire of 89
Lyell, Dr Richard 78

Macaulay, T. B. 48
Maguire, J. R., 48
Maidstone, Kent, College 8; Palace 8, 17
Mason, Sir John 78
Massyngham, John, sculptor 5, 6
Medehill, John, clerk of works 5
Mengs, Raphael, artist 52
Mews, Sir Peter 38, 84
Miller, Sanderson, architect 49 n.
Mocket, Richard, Warden 80

Napper, Edward 78
Niblett, Stephen, Warden 47

Offley, Revd. Francis 83
Otford Palace, Kent 17
Oxford:
  All Souls College passim
  Balliol College 12
  Barford Hall 2
  Brasenose College 12
  Carfax Conduit 81
  Cathedral 65
  Charlton's Hall or Inn 2, 3
  Christ Church 12
    Tom Tower 44
  Corpus Christi College 12
  Divinity School 16
  Exeter College 65
  Hart Hall 87
  Martyrs' Memorial 65
  Merton College 5, 6, 9, 12, 59, 79, 82
  New College 2, 9, 12, 15, 16
  Oseney Abbey 4
  Radcliffe Library 19, 41, 90
  Radcliffe Square 30, 41, 58, 90
  Rose Inn 79
  Rose Well 79
  St Bernard's College 1, 12, 16
  St John's Entry 3
  St Thomas Hall 3, 4
  Studley's Entry 4
  Tingewick's Inn 15
Oxford Architects' Partnership 73

Palmer, Thomas 84
Parker, Matthew, Archbishop of Canterbury 80
Petre, Sir William 78, 79
Pole ('Poole'), David, Bishop of Peterborough 78
Pope, John 78
Portman, Henry Seymour- see Seymour-Portman, Henry
Portman, Sir William 83
Potter, John 15

Radcliffe, Dr John 30, 90
Risborough, Bucks. 6
Robarts, C. H. 57–8, 73
Roberts, Thomas, plasterer 33, 52
Robertson, Daniel, architect 54, 56
Rouse, John 2

Salisbury, 3rd Marquis of 65 n.
Salter, H. E. 3, 4
Santini see Aichl
Scamozzi, Vincenzo, architect 21
Scott, Sir George Gilbert, architect 65–70
Seymour-Portman, Henry 83
Shadwell, Sir John 83
Shotover, Oxon. 6
Smith, George 79
Sneyd, Lewis, Warden 47, 70
Snow, Ralph 82
Soane, Sir John, architect 54

Stafford, John, Archbishop of Canterbury 13, 80 n.
Stewart, William, General 32, 84
Stokeley, Roger, Warden 78
Stow Wood, Oxon. 6
Studley Priory, Oxon. 4

Talbot of Hensol, Charles, 1st Baron 84
Talbot, Gilbert 49
Talman, John, architect 24
Tanner, Thomas, Bishop of St Asaph 83, 84
Taynton, Oxon., quarry 5, 6
Terry, Henry, sculptor 70 n.
Thornhill, Sir James, artist 58, 63, 83
Totternhoe, Beds., stone, 6
Townesend, William, mason 24–46 *passim*
Tracy, John, Viscount, Warden 47
Trevor, Thomas, 2nd Baron 84

Valdés Leal, Juan de, painter 52
Vanbrugh, Sir John, architect 27, 46

Vansittart, Robert 49, 72

Wakeman, H. O. 70
Waldoe, Revd. P. 83
Wanstead House, Essex 24
Warner, John, Warden 78–9
Webb, John, architect 23
Webb, John, fellow of All Souls 83
Wharton, Philip, Duke of 33, 84
White, Charlotte 58–9
White, Henry 82
Wilcox, Edward, carpenter 24
Williams, Roger 83
Williams, William 42, 43
Willis, Richard, Bishop of Winchester 84
Wood, Dr Robert 83
Wren, Sir Christopher, architect 44, 58, 70
Wyatt, Thomas 56–8
Wykeham, William of, Bishop of Winchester 2, 17
Wynne, J. H. 49